YOUR ULTIMATE CALLING

Other Hay House Books by Dr. Wayne W. Dyer

YOUR ULTIMATE CALLING

365 Ways to Bring Inspiration into Your Life

Dr. Wayne W. Dyer

HAY HOUSE, INC.

Carlsbad, California • New York City
London • Sydney • Johannesburg
Vancouver • Hong Kong • New Delhi

Published and distributed in the United States by: Hay House, Inc.: www.hayhouse.com • *Published and distributed in Australia by:* Hay House Australia Pty. Ltd.: www.hayhouse.com.au • *Published and distributed in the United Kingdom by:* Hay House UK, Ltd.: www.hayhouse.co.uk • *Published and distributed in the Republic of South Africa by:* Hay House SA (Pty), Ltd.: www.hayhouse.co.za • *Distributed in Canada by:* Raincoast: www.raincoast.com • *Published in India by:* Hay House Publishers India: www.hayhouse.co.in

Editorial supervision: Jill Kramer • *Design:* Charles McStravick
Production assistance: Alexandra Cardarelli

The material in this book was adapted from the *Inspiration Perpetual Flip Calendar,* by Dr. Wayne W. Dyer (Hay House, Inc., 2007).

Library of Congress Control Number: 2006921538

ISBN: 978-1-4019-1224-6

11 10 09 08   5 4 3 2
1st edition, May 2008
2nd edition, May 2008

Printed in China

INTRODUCTION

"What I'm offering here is the awareness that we can return to a full-time position

of inspiration,

which is the true meaning of our life."

I've put together this book because I know without any doubt that inspiration can be cultivated and be a driving force throughout life, rather than showing up every now and then and just as mysteriously disappearing, seemingly independent of our desires. Inspiration is for everyone! It isn't reserved for high-profile creative geniuses in the arts and sciences—it's inherent in our Divine birthright.

As you read each of the entries within these pages, you'll find specific suggestions for living *in-Spirit*. I'm offering you a blueprint through the world of inspiration—*your ultimate calling.*

— Dr. Wayne W. Dyer

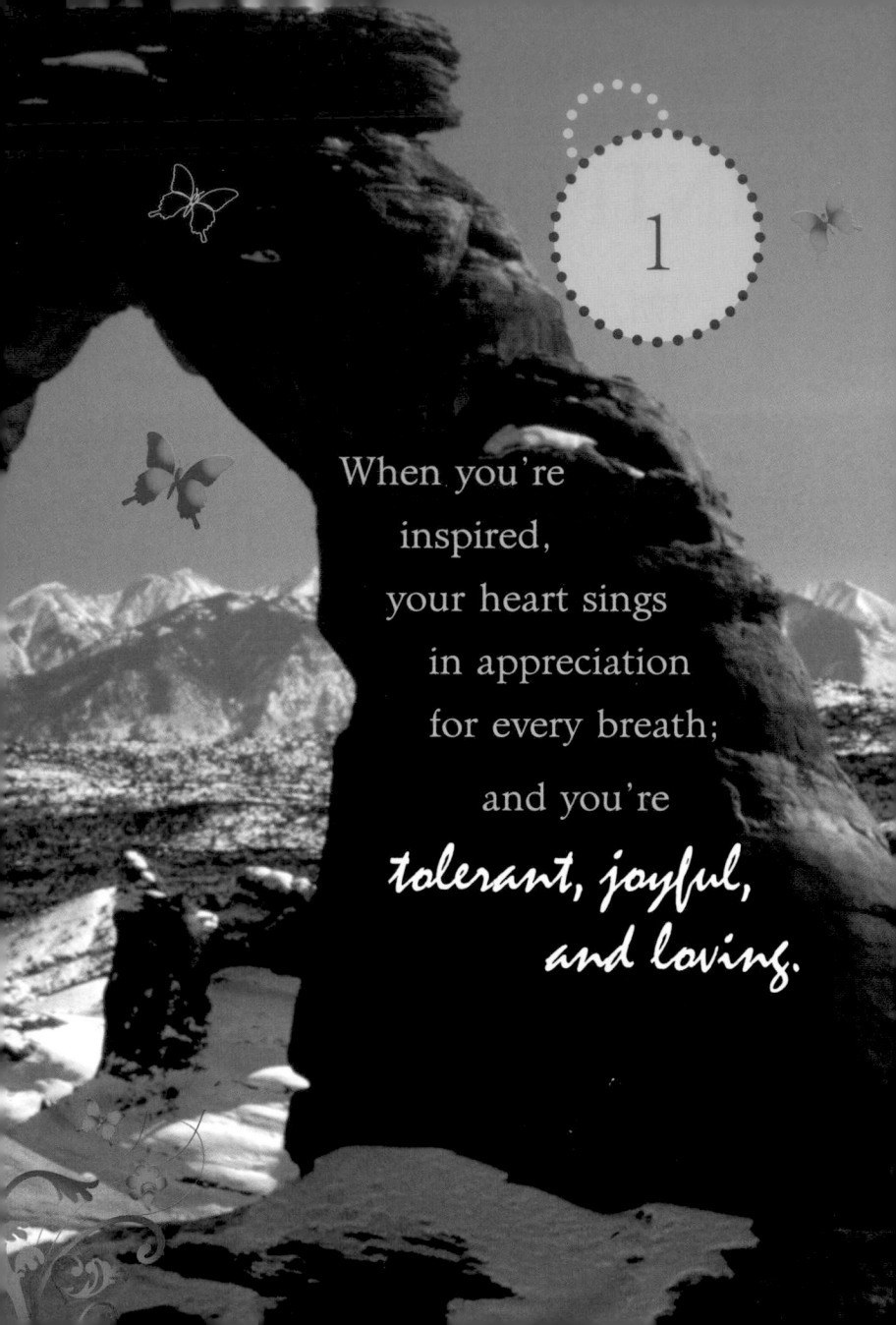

1

When you're
inspired,
your heart sings
in appreciation
for every breath;
and you're

*tolerant, joyful,
and loving.*

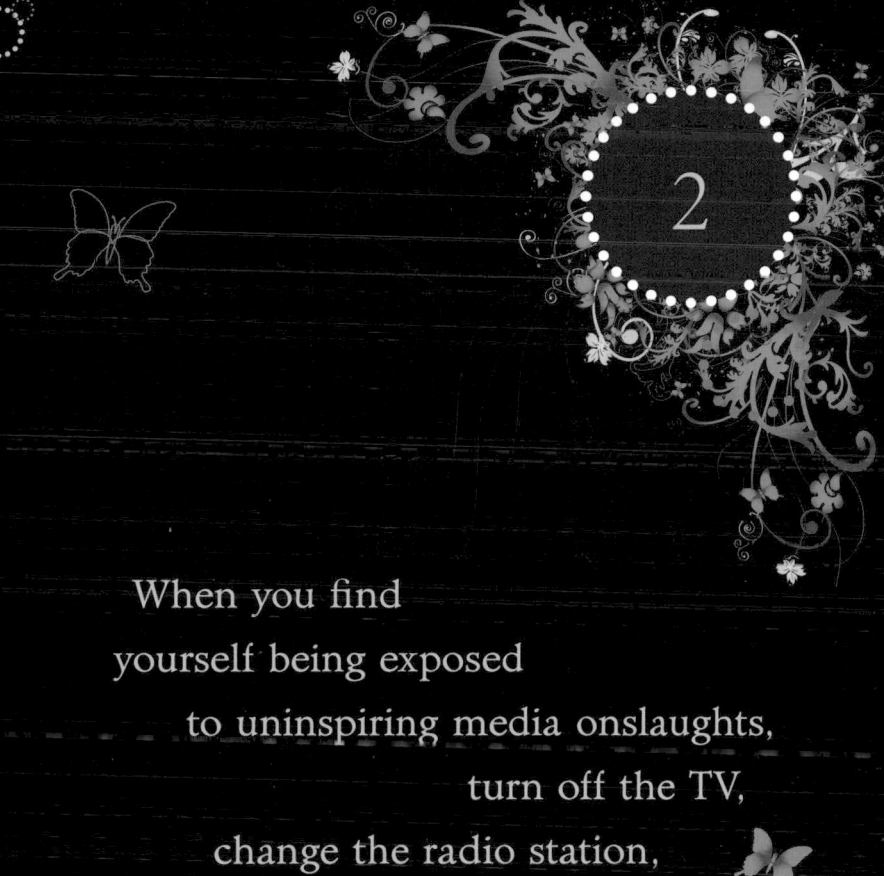

2

When you find
yourself being exposed
to uninspiring media onslaughts,
turn off the TV,
change the radio station,
put the magazine down,
and affirm: *I no longer wish to be
in the energy field of anything
that isn't a **vibrational match**
with Spirit.*

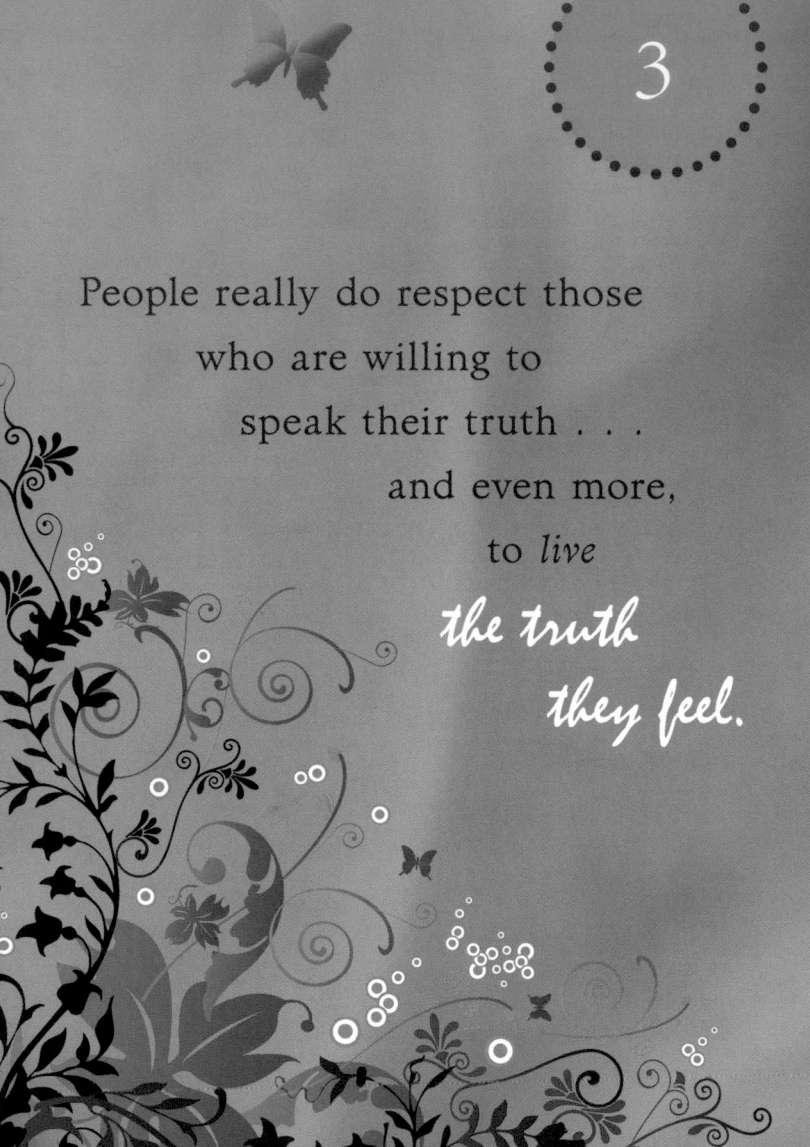

3

People really do respect those
who are willing to
speak their truth . . .
and even more,
to *live*

*the truth
they feel.*

4

When you were *in-Spirit* prior to materializing, your aim was high and your expectations were *Godlike.* Reacquaint yourself with that *vision.*

5

By training your memory,
you'll be able to return to
early childhood recollections
of love, peace, and joy—
and back even further to your origins.
You might discover that you have more
access to your past and your
spiritual beginnings than you might
have believed.

6

Be cognizant
of how the God-force
has delivered
many blessings to you
throughout your life
and continues
to do so.

7

Before beginning your day,
*spend some time
with God*
during the early morning.
When you wake up,
say to yourself, *These are my few
moments with God.*
In these moments
reflect, feel the peace,
and most important,
express your
gratitude.

8

Extend some kind of *unexpected generosity* to another person, preferably a stranger, every single day for two weeks. The more you practice being generous, the more you'll impact others in an inspiring way.

9

Anticipate
a world at peace.
Expect health, abundance,
and love
in your life and in the lives
of others.

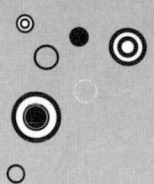

10

When you remember
to summon the

well-being of God

and know that you're always
connected to this Source,
it is then that
you're said to be inspired.

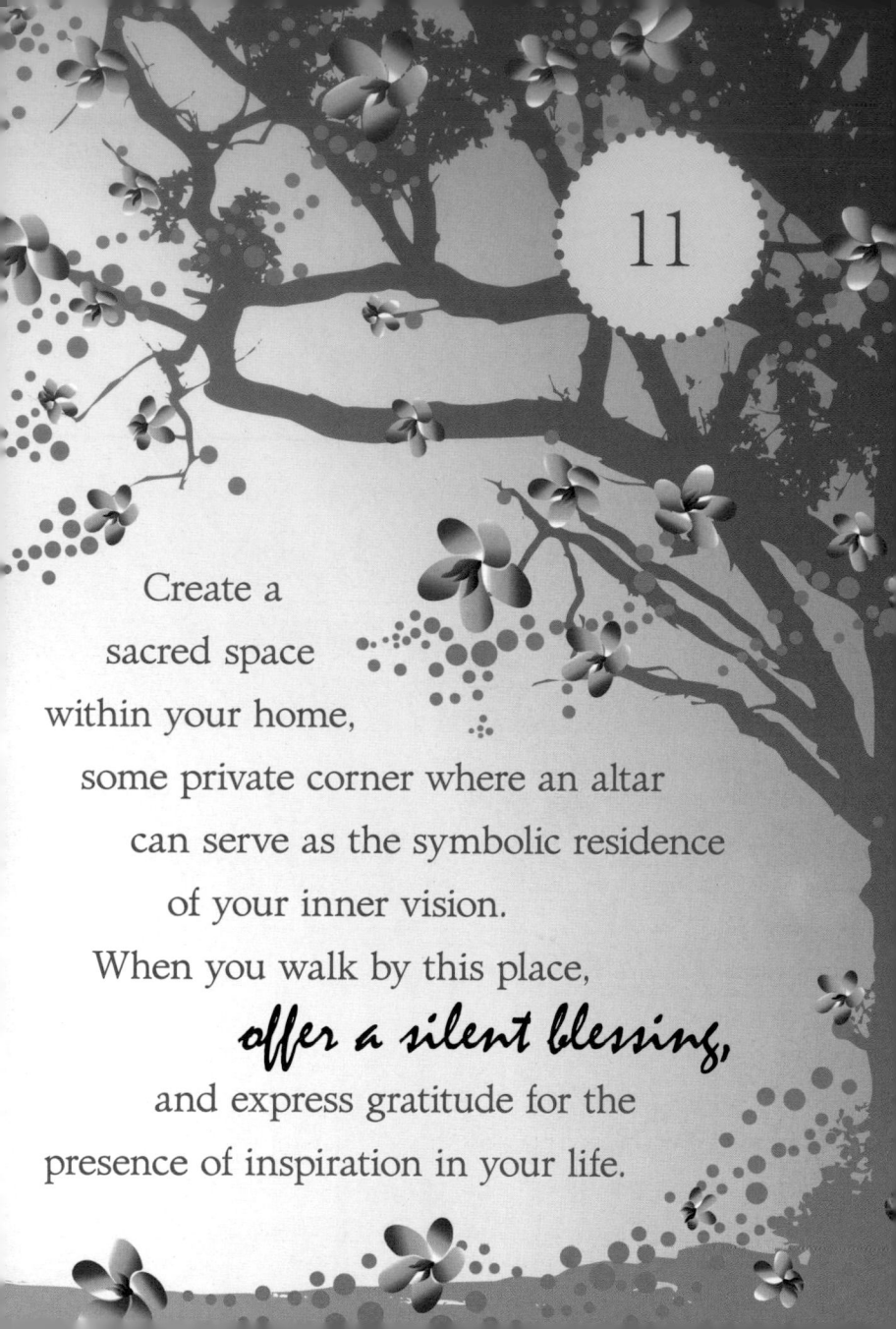

11

Create a
sacred space
within your home,
some private corner where an altar
can serve as the symbolic residence
of your inner vision.
When you walk by this place,
offer a silent blessing,
and express gratitude for the
presence of inspiration in your life.

The willingness to
listen and act on
your inspiration,
independent of the opinions of others,
is imperative if you're going
to live the life you desire.

12

13

Keep in mind that
you're not being cruel
by destroying your ego,
since it's a
false self
to begin with.

14

Choose to associate with
people who live their lives,
for the most part, *in-Spirit*.
But first you need to identify
those who are inspired and inspiring—
individuals who've

risen above their egos

and the vanities of the world.

15

Affirm

over and over

throughout the day:

I attract peace, not conflict.

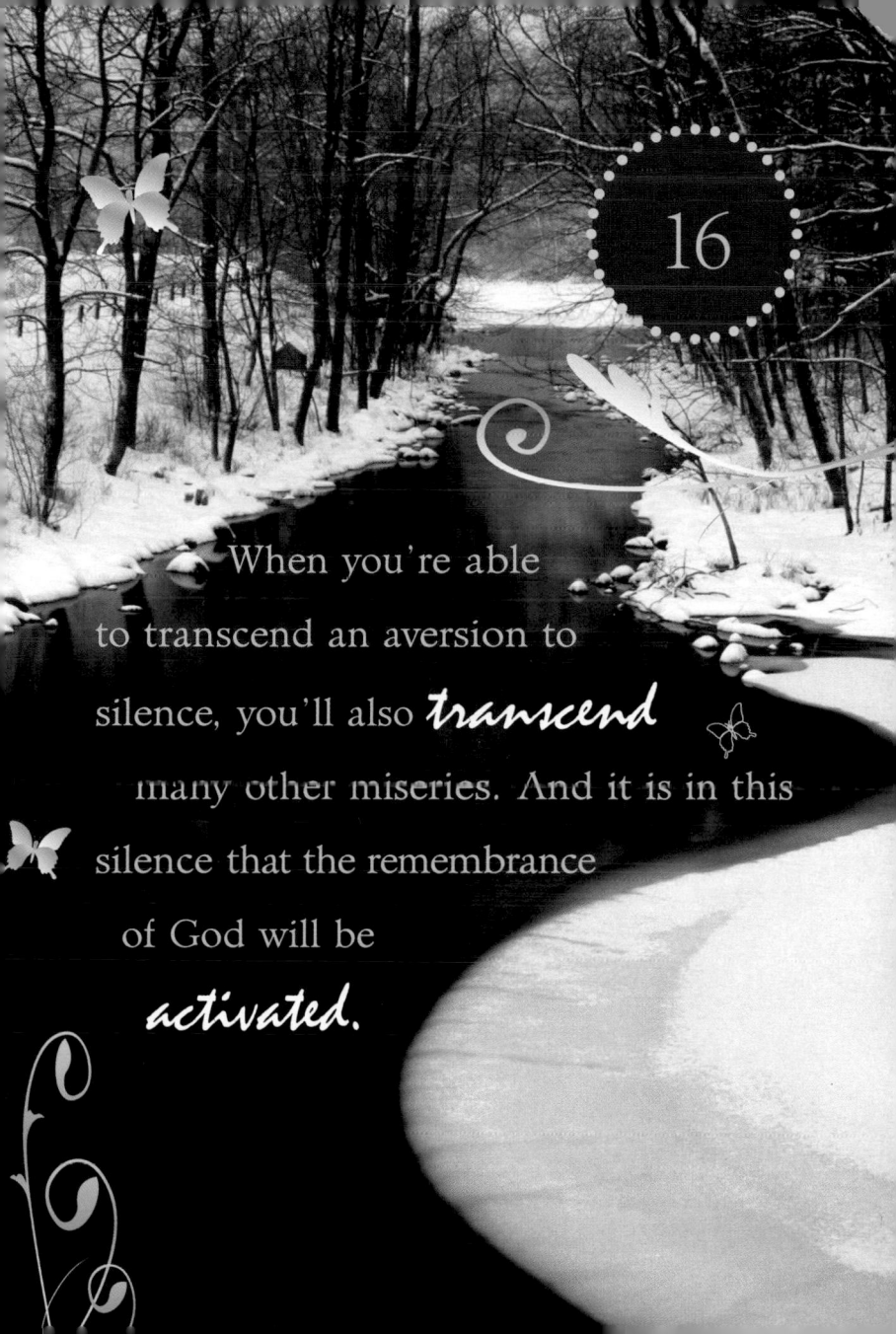

16

When you're able to transcend an aversion to silence, you'll also *transcend* many other miseries. And it is in this silence that the remembrance of God will be *activated.*

17

Listen to the wind,
the critters,
the rain,
and the ocean.
Listen to it all.

18

When you're enthusiastically
living your passion,
whatever it may be,
you transmit spiritual signals
to those around you that you're *in-Spirit*—
loving who you are,
what you came here to be,
and whoever comes
into your field of vision.

19

Try to *free yourself*
from placing a cash value
on everything you
have, do, and say.
*Doing what your heart
tells you*
will bring you joy,
rather than determining
whether it will
be cost-effective.

20

In the private,

quiet moments

when you ask for

Divine assistance,

you might pray like this:

Dear God,

make me an instrument of Thy love.

I want to be like You.

I have forgiven them,

and I have forgiven myself.

21

Know that for every act
of apparent evil,
there are a million acts of kindness,
and that's where you need
to focus your attention.

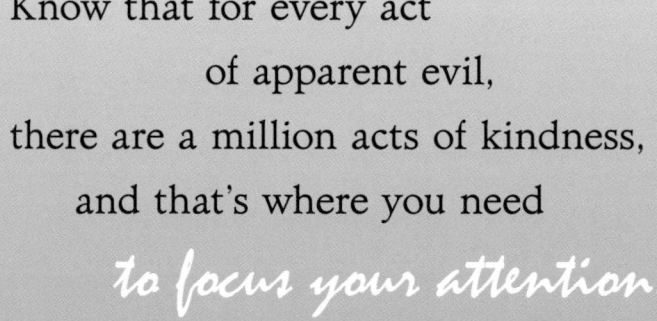

22

When you think thoughts that are *in-Spirit*,
they reflect a vibrational alignment

that moves you in the *right* direction.
But if you begin observing
your thoughts and realize
that you're going

in the *wrong* direction,
*you can make
a U-turn with
new thoughts.*

23

Pay attention
to episodes in nature
that kindle an inner spark
of awe and admiration.
You don't have to discuss it
with another being.
If it has meaning to you,
it's valid.

24

As you move into
the world of inspiration,
you'll find it easy—

and even necessary—
to give thanks

for all of the people in your life,
and to take serious note
of what they brought you.

The quality
that stands out
among those who feel inspired
is one of intense, burning desire.
The intensity of this desire
needs to be so great that your love
for who you are and what you do
precludes the possibility
of any boredom, tedium,
or weariness.

25

26

It is Spirit that gives life.

You came from Spirit

and are like

what you came from.

27

Becoming inspired
requires that you be
curious about, and attentive to,
feelings that emerge
to help you reconnect
with your original self.

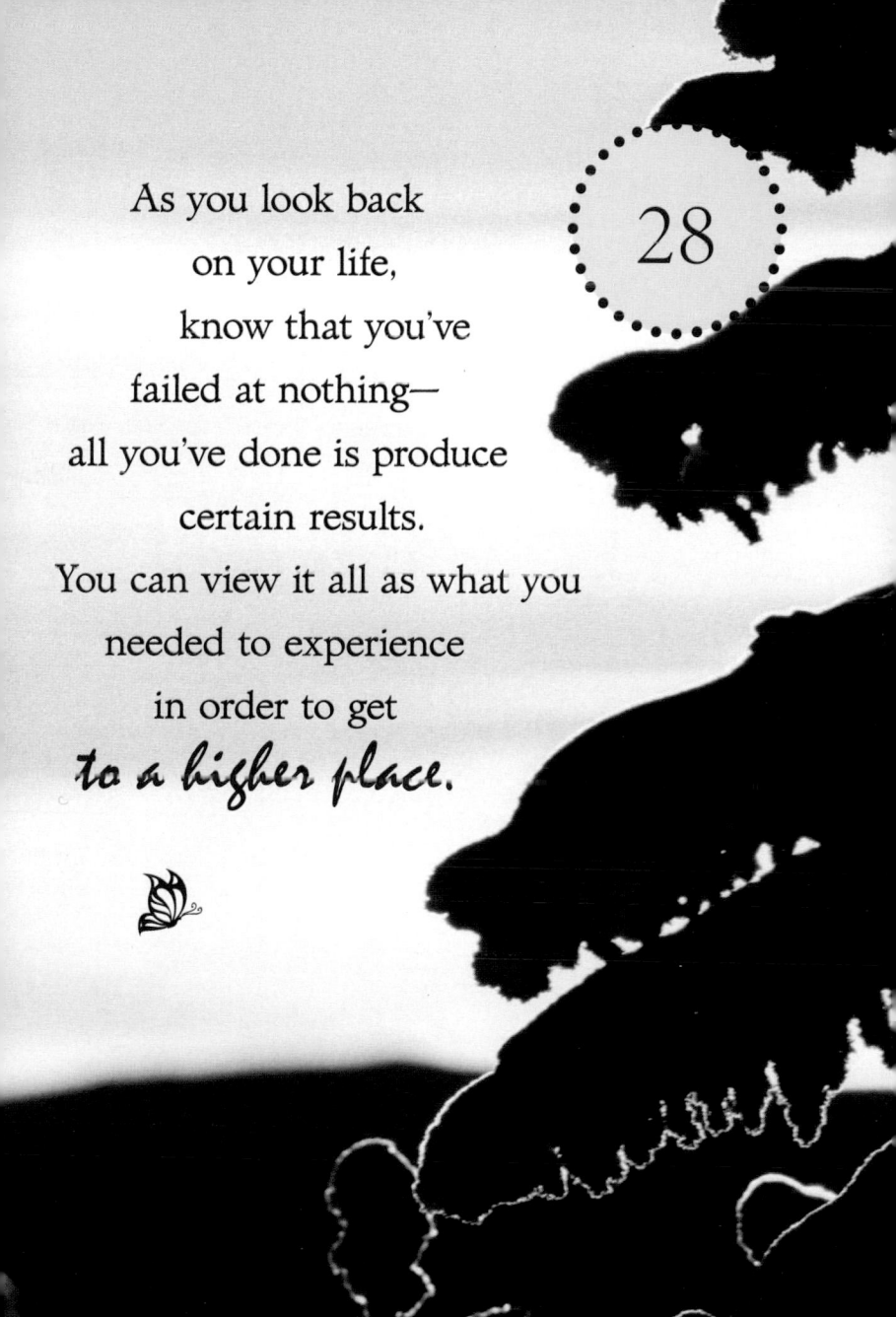

28

As you look back
on your life,
know that you've
failed at nothing—
all you've done is produce
certain results.
You can view it all as what you
needed to experience
in order to get
to a higher place.

29

When you're inspired,
*you're not judging others
or yourself.*
You aren't bothered by
behaviors or attitudes
that in uninspired moments
are frustrating.

30

Abandonment, abuse,
and disloyalty
can be valuable teachers
when you see
that you experienced them for a
greater good.

Notice incidents
such as banging your elbow
or stubbing your toe.
Stop in those moments
and ask yourself,
What was I just thinking,
and how is it related to
what appeared to be an accident?
Doing so *creates*
a constant awareness
of your Source
and the direction
of your life.

Change your expectations for yourself:

Expect the best,

expect Divine guidance,

expect your fortunes to change . . .

expect a miracle.

33

Keeping life simple
means having faith
that your spiritual connection
flourishes in a life dedicated to joy,
love, and peace.
If your daily activities
are so overwhelming
that you
don't make
these things your priority,
you're disregarding
the value of

living a simple life.

34

If you've been addicted
to a harmful substance,
to overeating,
or even to being a doormat,
listen to the voice within
that begs you
to take just
one corrective step.

35

Before speaking,
*consult your
inner-truth barometer,*
and resist the temptation
to tell people only what
they want to hear.

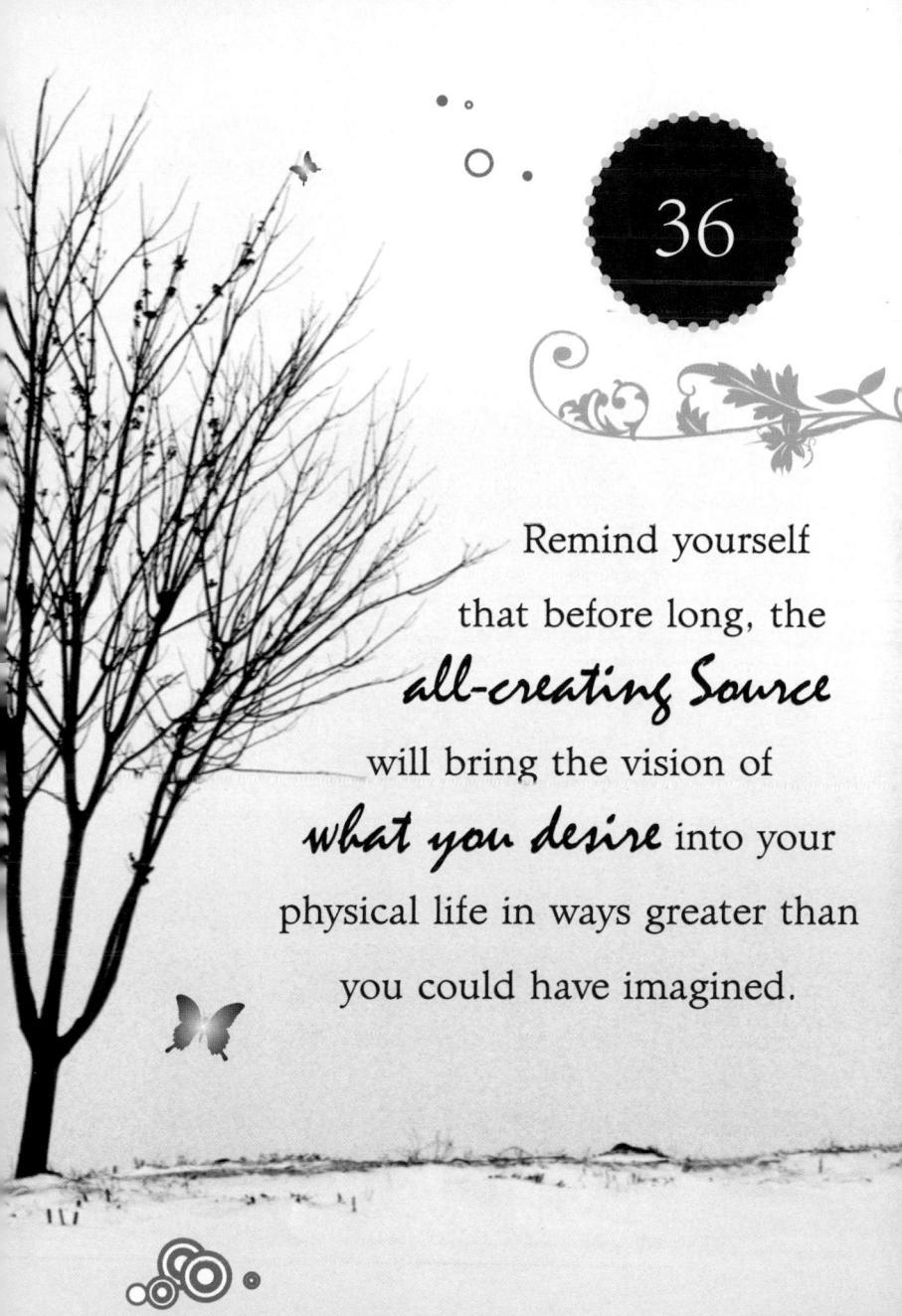

36

Remind yourself that before long, the *all-creating Source* will bring the vision of *what you desire* into your physical life in ways greater than you could have imagined.

37

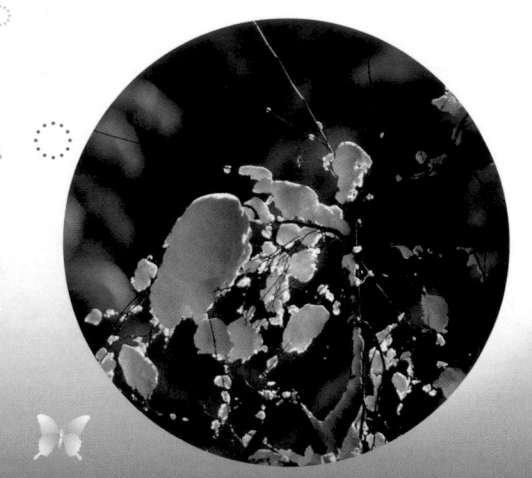

Don't assume that
just because God is all-knowing,
every problem is going
to be handled for you.
Remind yourself that you're a *co*-Creator.

You're a piece of God.

Being inspired
means that you're willing

*to act upon your
inner impulses*

so that you'll never experience
the pain of dying
while still wondering,
What if . . . ?

38

39

When you're *in-Spirit*,
you have no need for the ego
and have no illusion
of being the false self.
Therefore, the ego
has no influence on you.

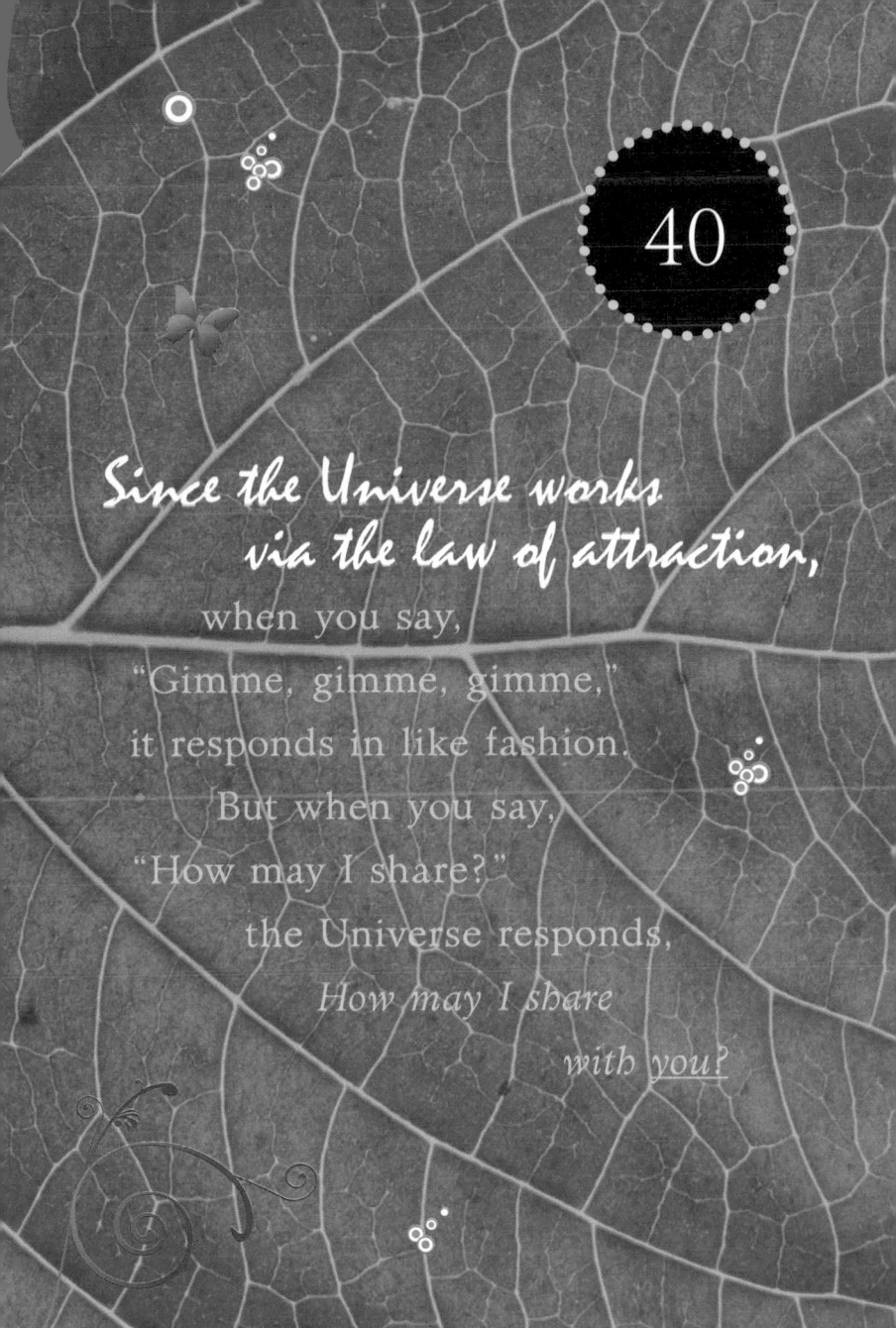

40

Since the Universe works
via the law of attraction,
when you say,
"Gimme, gimme, gimme,"
it responds in like fashion.
But when you say,
"How may I share?"
the Universe responds,
How may I share
with you?

41

Monitor your thoughts
for any that put bonds
on your ability to manifest.
Even a seemingly insignificant one
that questions your resolve
to live *in-Spirit* represents
an energy vibration
that inhibits you
from creating
your desires.

42

You don't need more of anything
to become inspired;
rather, you need to take
your attention away from what you
see and move into
the miraculous world of Spirit,
where joy and bliss
await you.

43

Know that your thoughts—
which emerge as interests,
excitement, inner thrills,
and illuminating sensations—
are indications that you have
the necessary ability
*to merge
with your
magnificent creativity.*

44

When you're inspired,

you're totally engaged in the now.

In a never-beginning
and never-ending
Universe,
there is no past.

45

When you think about
others before yourself
and offer the love
you feel for all of life—
first in your thoughts
and then in your actions—
that's how you make
*a connection
to inspiration.*

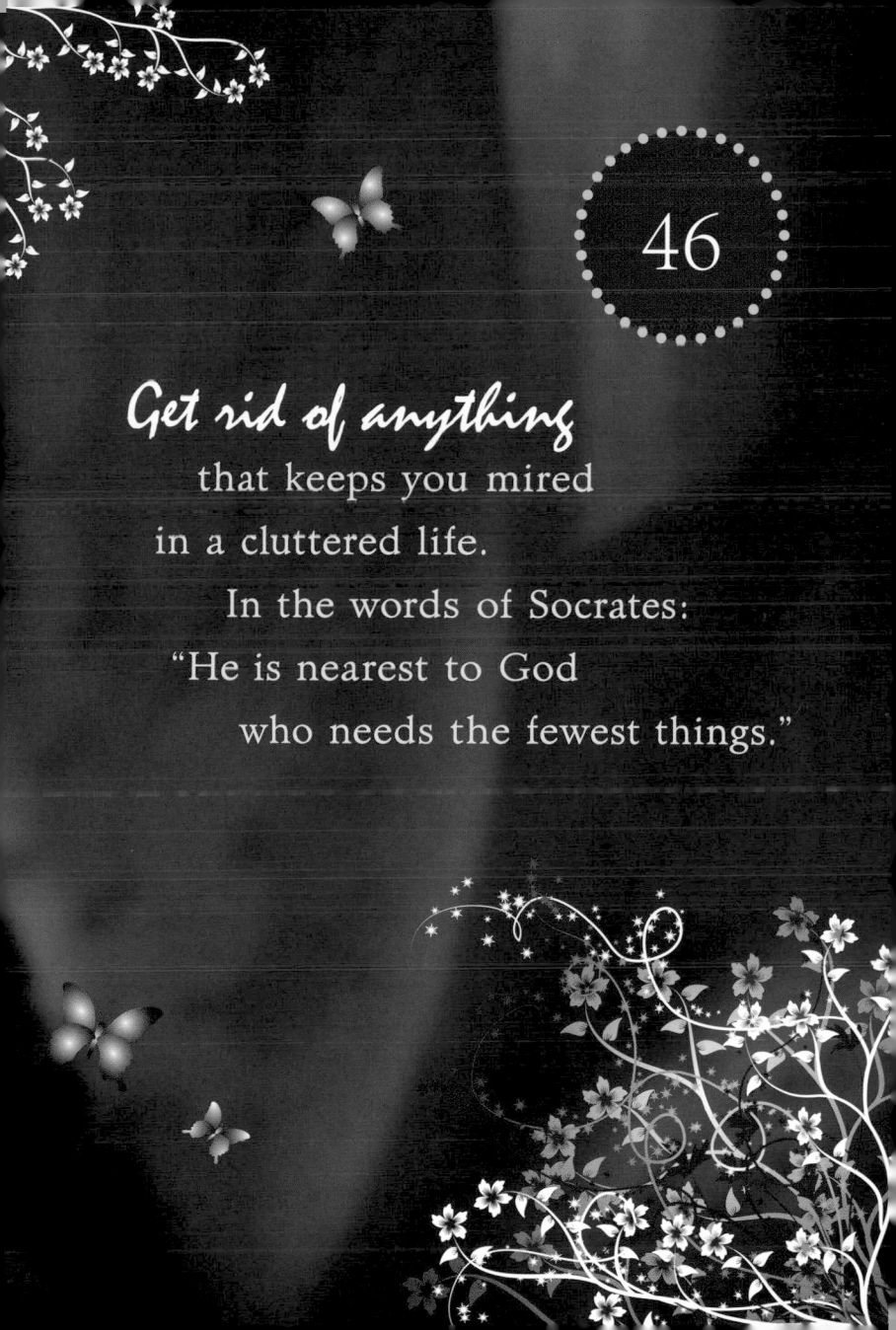

46

Get rid of anything
that keeps you mired
in a cluttered life.
In the words of Socrates:
"He is nearest to God
who needs the fewest things."

47

You need to awaken

from the bad dream

that has stupefied you in the fog of ego,

and live from

the blissful perspective

offered by being *in-Spirit*.

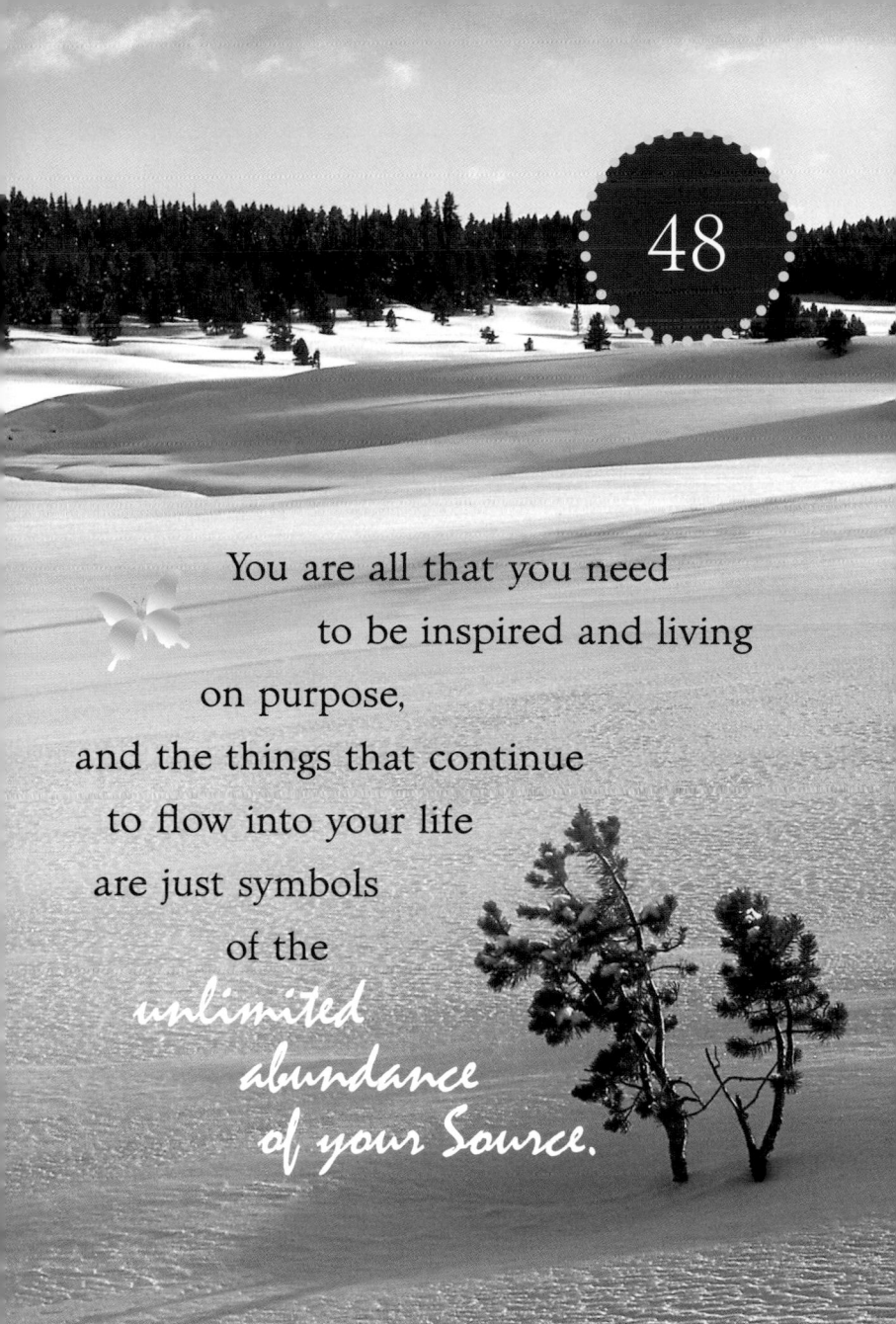

48

You are all that you need
to be inspired and living
on purpose,
and the things that continue
to flow into your life
are just symbols
of the
unlimited
abundance
of your Source.

49

It's imperative to
eliminate self-perceptions
that might cloud your vision or
make you question your
*Divine
magnificence.*

50

Regardless of your
current station in life,
you have a
spiritual contract
to make joy your constant
companion.

51

When a book literally falls into your lap
or is sent to you by
several different people—
or even when you keep seeing
the title and having it referred to by
others over and over—
you need to notice,
*stop your resistance,
and surrender.*

52

When you remember
to stay *in-Spirit*,
you'll realize that
when one thing appears
to be going wrong,
you can see clearly that

ten things are going right.

53

Make it your intention
to always stay inspired and
live what your mind knows,
rather than only what
your eyes see.

54

If you ignore
inspiration's powerful attraction,
the result is personal
discomfort
or a sense of disconnection
from yourself.

Vow to have fewer conflicts in your life.
You came from no conflict,
so you can return there and
know heaven on Earth
by refusing to let your inner world
be conflicted
by anyone
at any time.

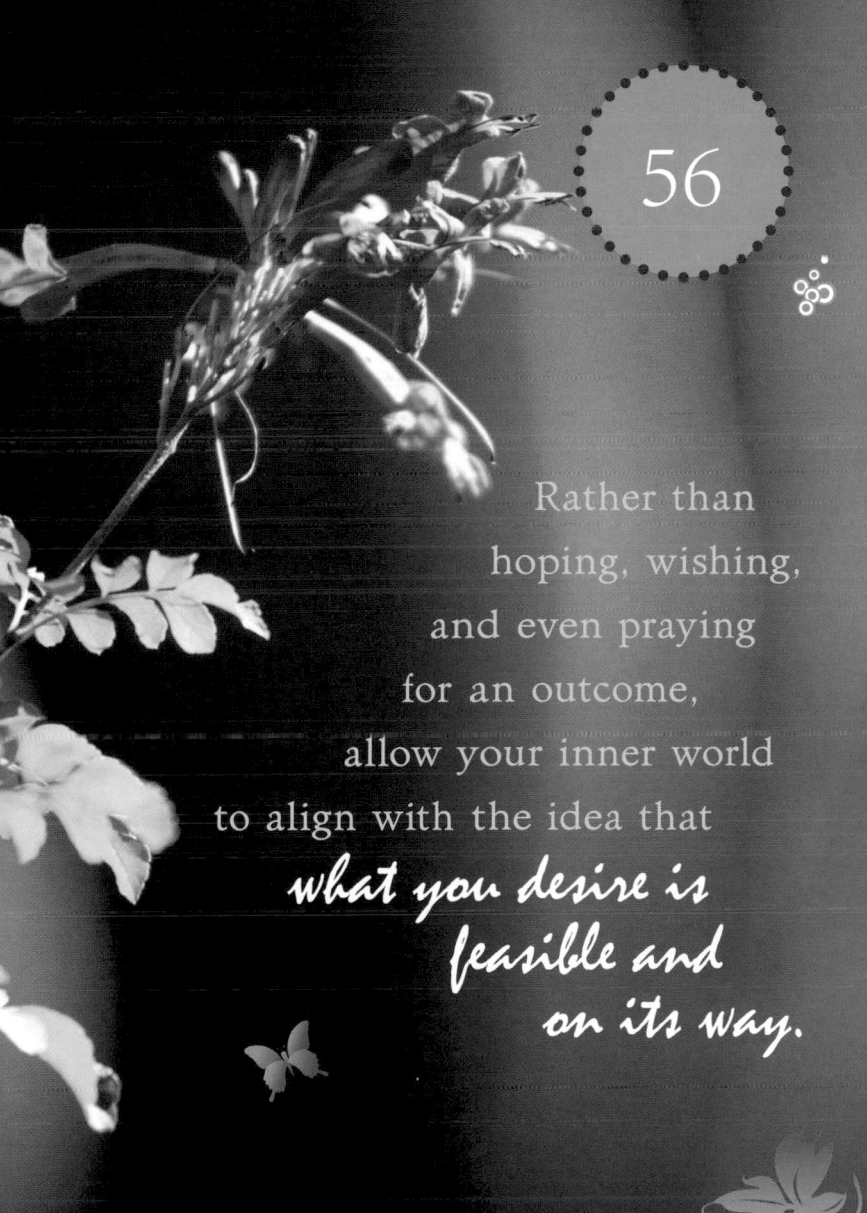

56

Rather than
hoping, wishing,
and even praying
for an outcome,
allow your inner world
to align with the idea that
*what you desire is
feasible and
on its way.*

57

Whenever you seem
to be receiving
an unexpected jolt
from the Universe,
make every effort
to note precisely
what it was that
you were thinking at the moment
you took in the message.

58

As you communicate

with your Source of Being,

know that you're

awakening a

part of yourself

that's just like it.

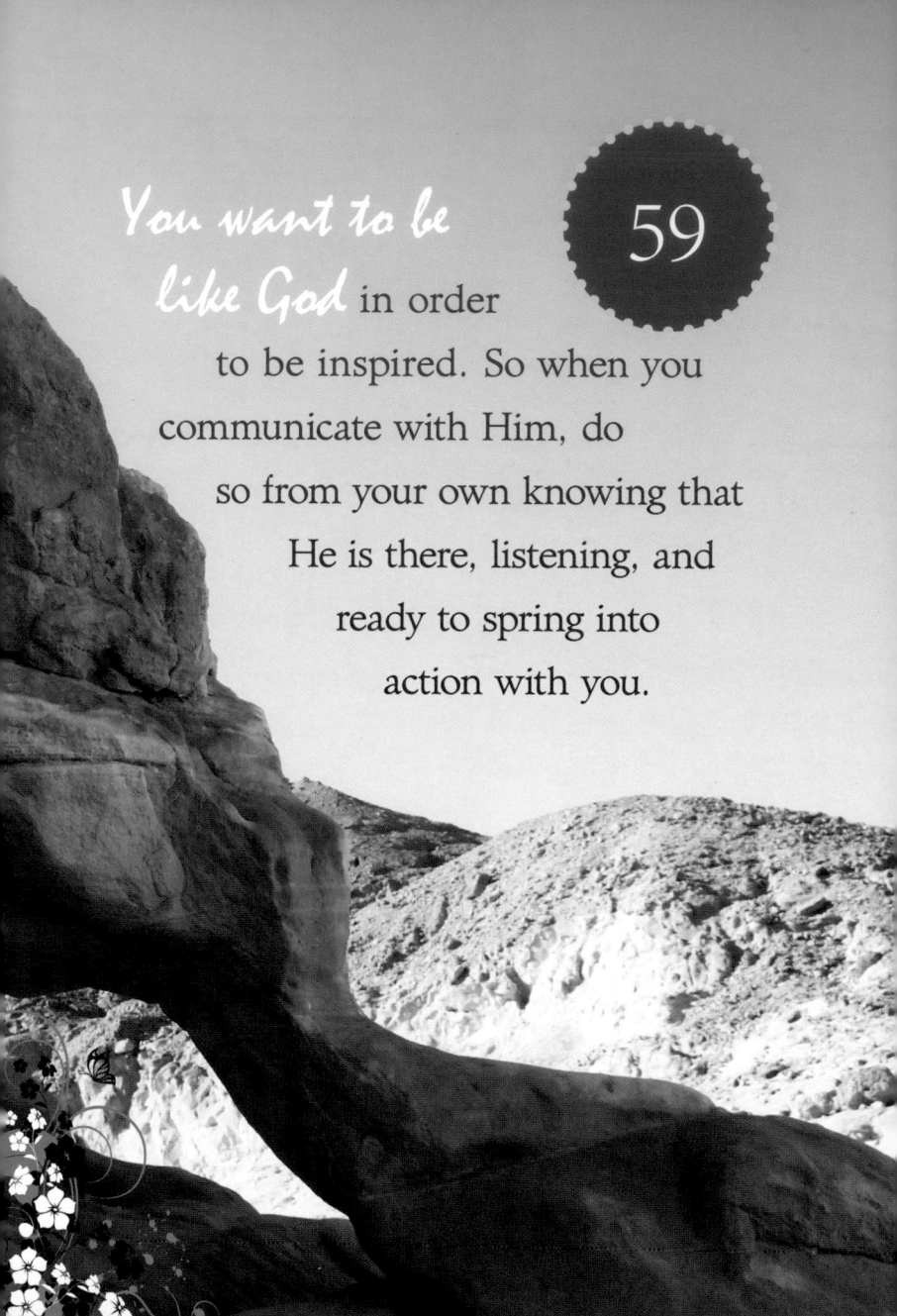

You want to be like God in order to be inspired. So when you communicate with Him, do so from your own knowing that He is there, listening, and ready to spring into action with you.

59

60

Accept no excuses:
Stop with the BS
and be truthful with yourself,
admit your flaws
rather than defending them,
and look in the mirror and
talk to yourself honestly.

61

Your weaknesses,
including your illnesses,
may come to you because
you're withholding something—
which could very well be your
*healthy, conscious
connection to Spirit.*

Write this down,

put it in a conspicuous place,

and repeat it to yourself:

I live in a Divinely inspired Universe.

I have nothing to fear.

I trust in myself, and when I do so,

I trust in the very Wisdom that created me.

63

Since everything you allow
into your life represents
an energy
that impacts you both
physically and spiritually,
it's imperative to raise
your awareness level

and defend against
the habits
that deter you
from being
in-Spirit.

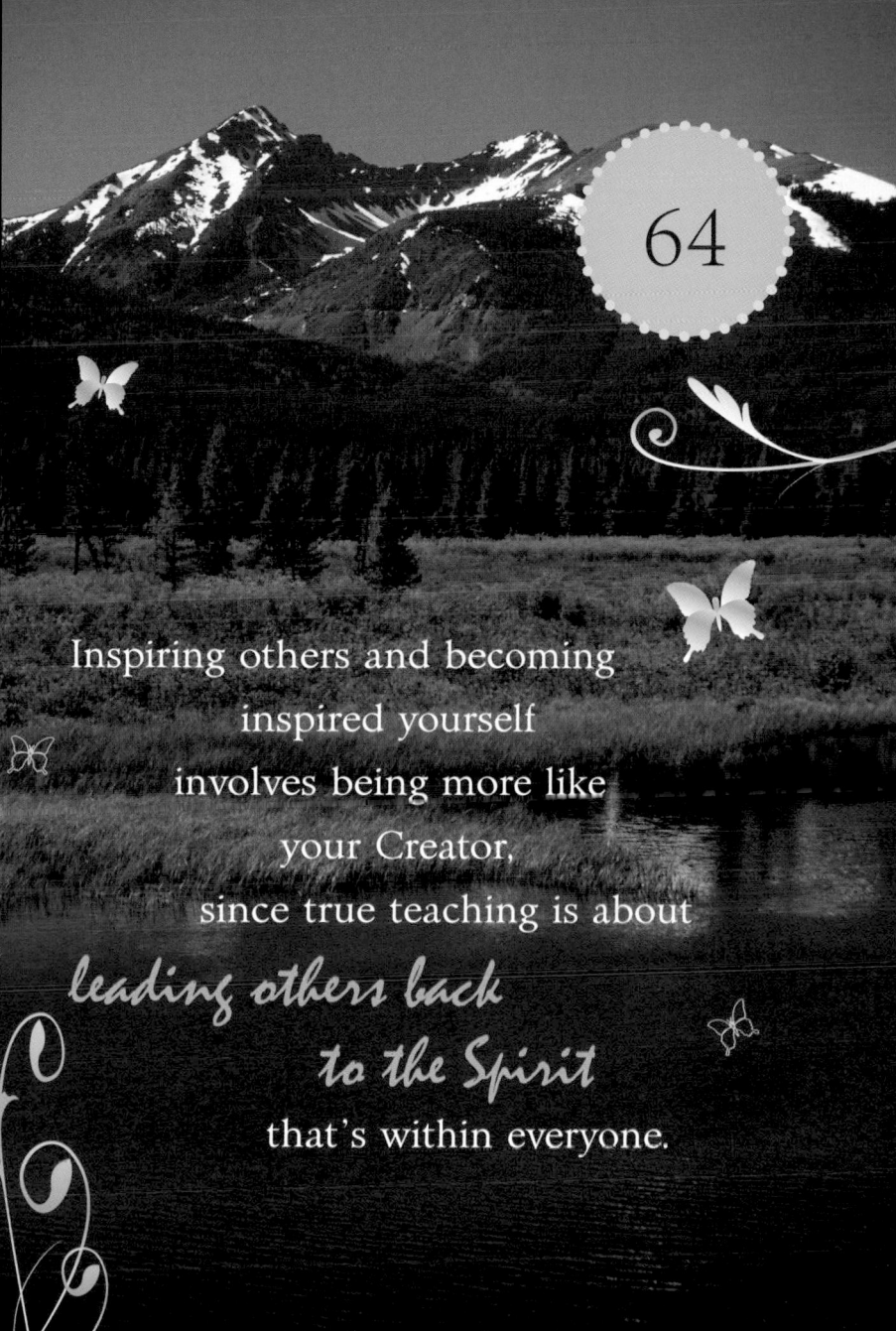

64

Inspiring others and becoming
inspired yourself
involves being more like
your Creator,
since true teaching is about
*leading others back
to the Spirit*
that's within everyone.

65

Make peace with silence,
and remind yourself
that it is in this space
that you'll come to
remember your Spirit.

66

In deep prayer,
you're not looking for the resolution
of conflict or answers
falling from the sky;
you just want to feel as if you're
in contact
with someone who
cares enough
to hear you out.

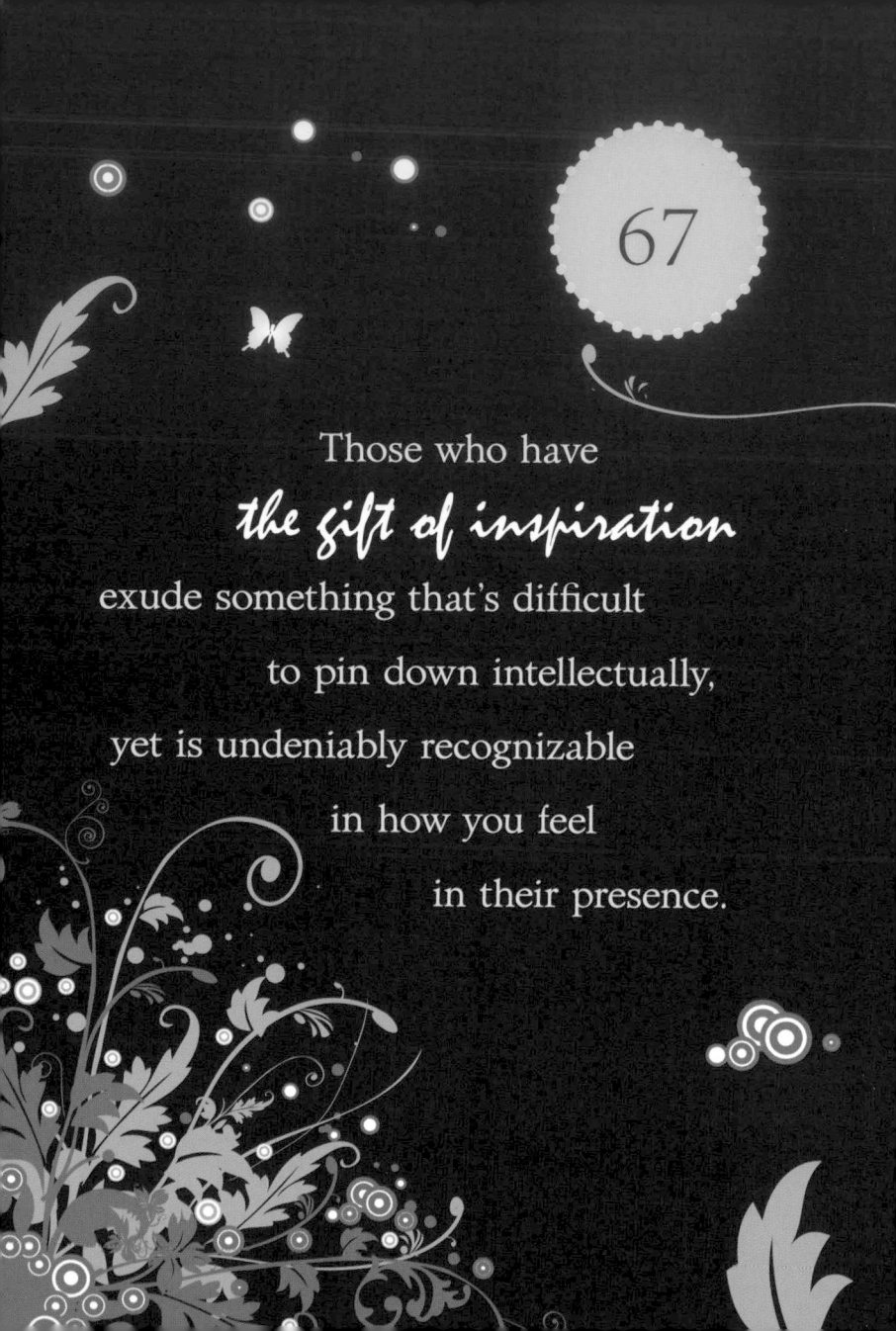

67

Those who have

the gift of inspiration

exude something that's difficult

to pin down intellectually,

yet is undeniably recognizable

in how you feel

in their presence.

68

Have faith.
Trust in a Universe
that's endless and endlessly creating.
Trust that the Creative Source of All
knows exactly
what It is doing.

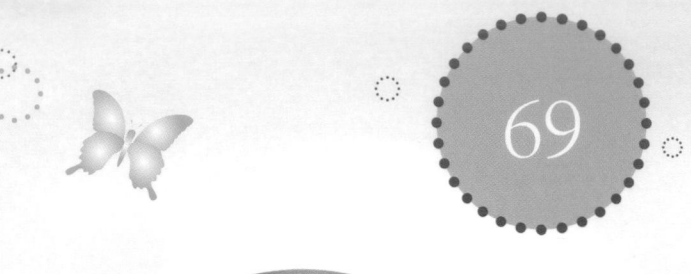

69

The power of an idea
whose time has come
*is really the power
of Spirit at work.*

70

You can go toward
  a clearer life
by examining and purifying
    your relationships
  with those you love,
  with yourself,
and with God.

71

Practice forgiveness every day.
The most difficult
or impossible situations
are the most essential!

72

Your thoughts about who you are,
what excites you,
and what you feel called to be and do
are all Divinely inspired
and come with whatever
guidance and assistance
you'll need to actualize
these goals.

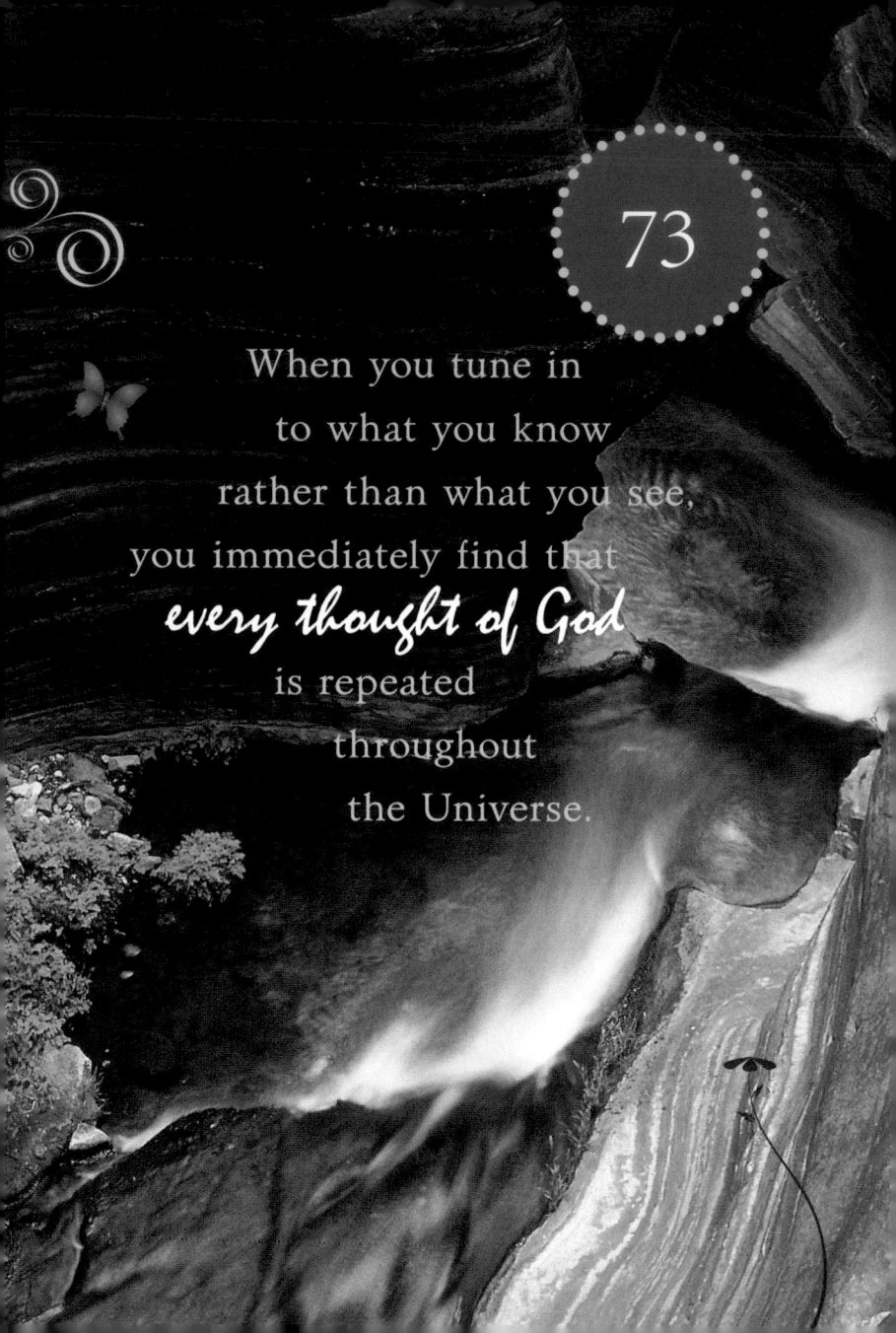

73

When you tune in
to what you know
rather than what you see,
you immediately find that
every thought of God
is repeated
throughout
the Universe.

74

**When you listen
and allow,
Spirit guides you.**
When you fail to listen,
or allow your ego to get in the way
and run the show,
you're no longer *in-Spirit* . . .
and are usually
uninspired.

75

It's vitally important

to hold a clear vision of yourself

as deserving of feeling inspired,

knowing that it's

your ultimate calling,

and choosing to be *in-Spirit*

even when everything

around you suggests

otherwise.

76

You must believe
in a Universe
that's created and guided
by an Intelligence
greater than your ego—
a Universe
*where there can be
no accidents.*

77

You have the free will
to choose either
to be or *not to be*
consciously
connected
with the
Creative
Spirit.

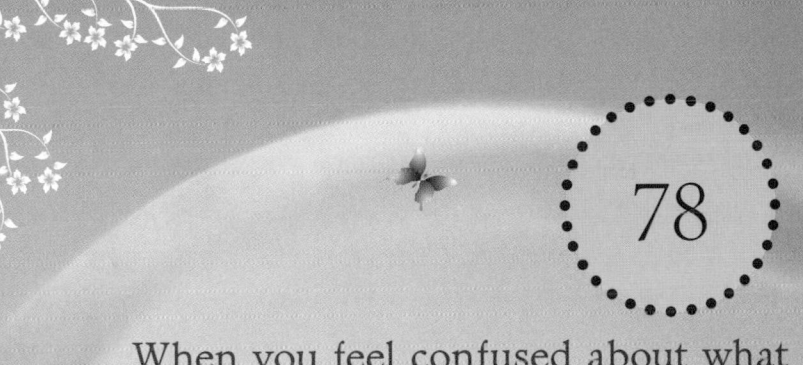

78

When you feel confused about what

you should do to feel inspired,

it's time to go to a quiet place.

It could be in your home,

down by the sea, in a meadow,

or deep in the woods—it just

needs to be somewhere you

can be alone

with God.

79

When you reemerge

into the perfect

oneness of Spirit,

you view everyone you meet

as an ally through your

inspired way of life.

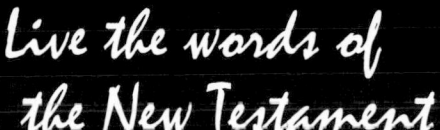

Live the words of the New Testament

80

that tell you that you're *in* this world but not *of* it. You can be here without being attached to being here by simply discarding your body identification.

81

See yourself as a single cell

in a body called humanity,

and vow to be a cell

that cooperates

with all adjacent cells

and has a

sense of belonging

to the whole.

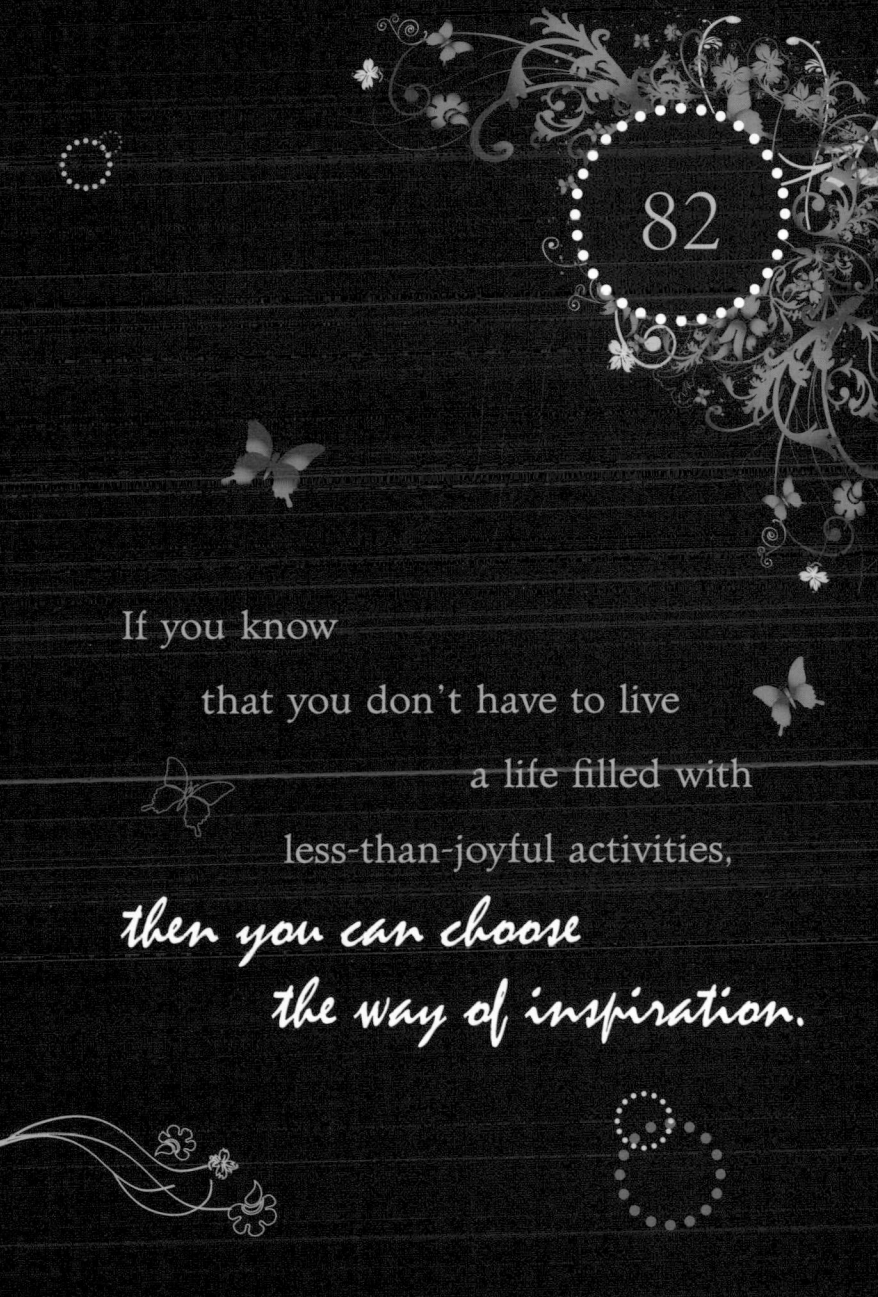

82

If you know
that you don't have to live
a life filled with
less-than-joyful activities,
*then you can choose
the way of inspiration.*

83

You are greatness personified,

a resident genius, and a creative master—

regardless of anyone's opinion.

Make a silent dedication to

encourage and express

your Divine nature.

84

Have faith

that whatever you need
to experience is on its way,
and that God won't send you anything
you're incapable of handling.
You can decide that the word *fear*
is an acronym for:
false evidence appearing real!

85

As your sense of inspiration
grows within you,
you'll find yourself wanting
to do more for others
and focusing less
upon yourself.

86

You have a built-in yearning to
seek your inspired self and feel
wholeness, a kind of
inexplicable sense that patiently
demands recognition and action.
You might describe it
as a mechanism persistently
projecting the words
destiny, mission,
or *purpose*
on your
inner screen.

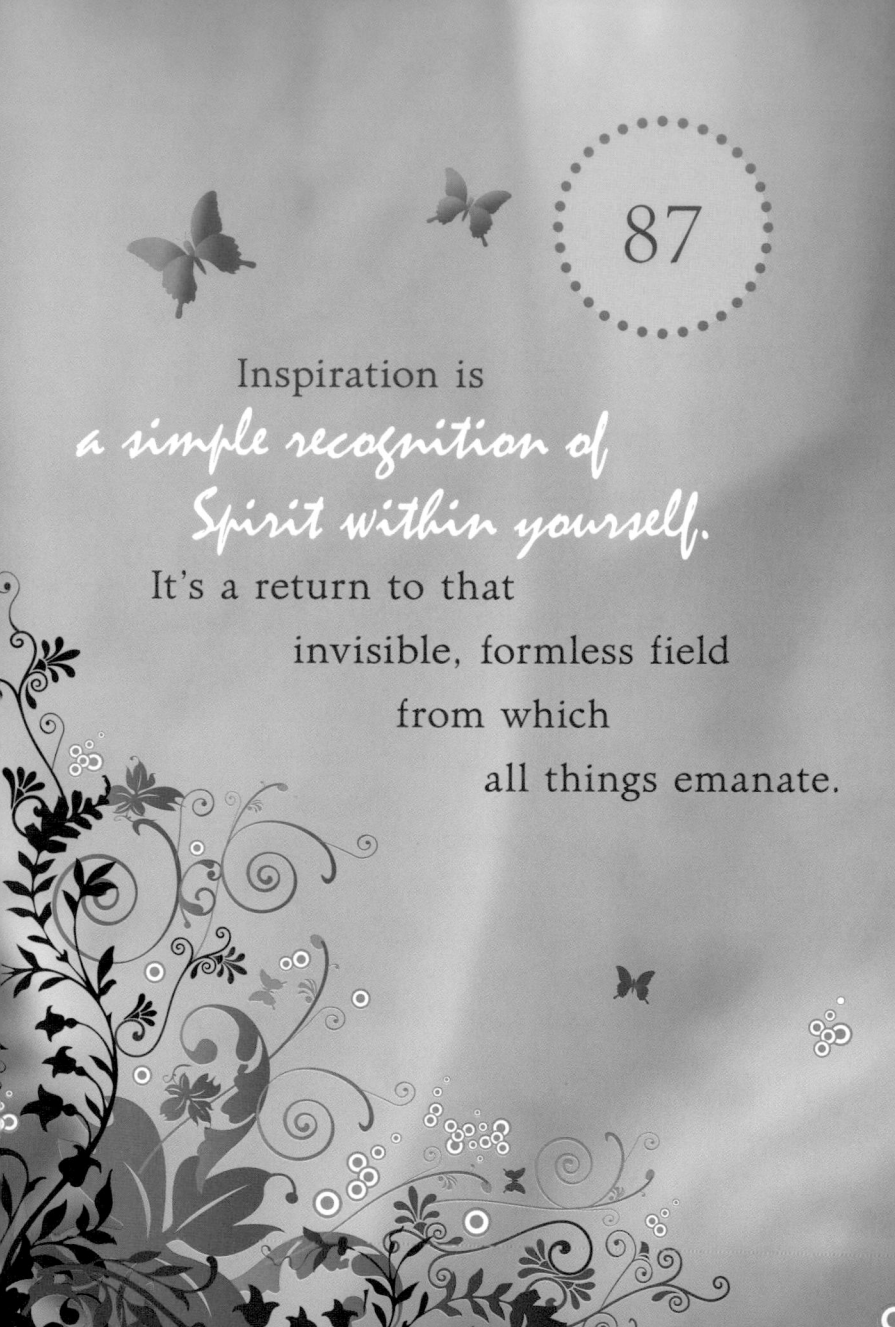

87

Inspiration is
*a simple recognition of
Spirit within yourself.*
It's a return to that
invisible, formless field
from which
all things emanate.

88

To become inspired

on a daily basis,
you must be able to
quickly identify any
thoughts that
are moving you
away from
your Source,
and then shift
the direction.

89

Being an example of
inner peace
is an effective way of
expressing your desire
to offer inspiration
to others.

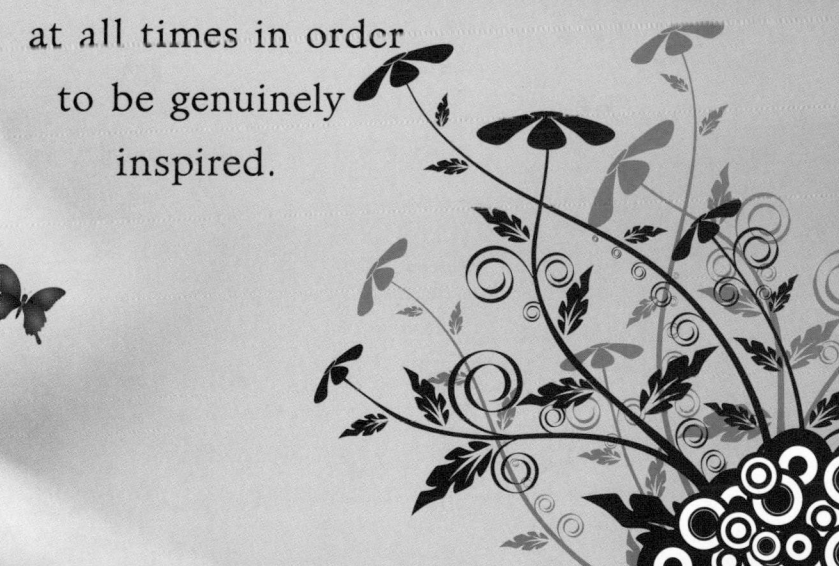

90

Your attitude toward your body,
along with how you feed and exercise it,
must match up with Spirit.
You came from love,
so you must extend that
love and appreciation to your body
at all times in order
to be genuinely
inspired.

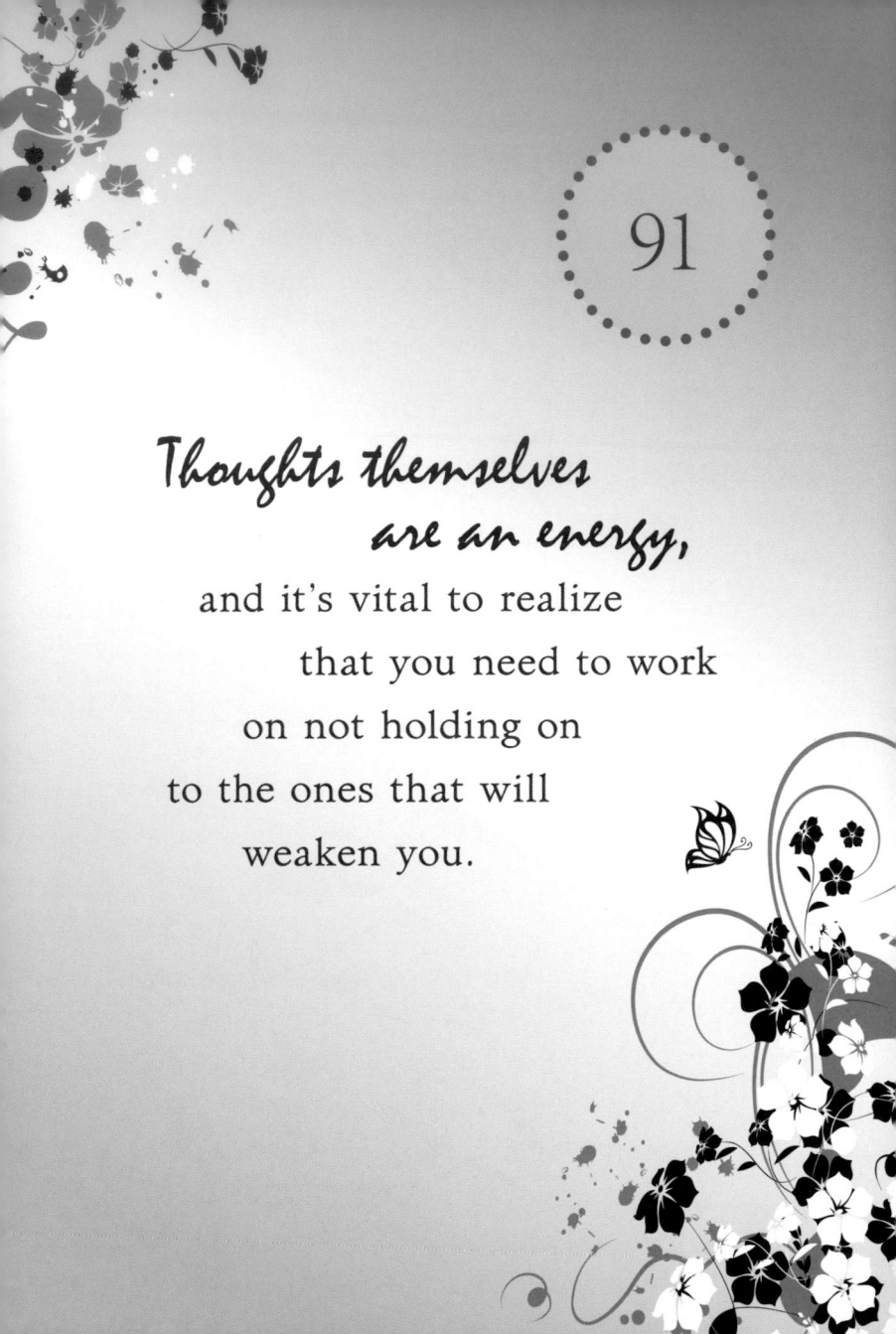

91

Thoughts themselves are an energy,

and it's vital to realize
that you need to work
on not holding on
to the ones that will
weaken you.

92

Work at
developing
your faith
each and every day
by taking time
to be quietly
in conscious contact
with the Creative Source
of your being.

93

Learn from Leo Tolstoy,
who said that
"the most difficult thing—
but an essential one—is to love Life,
to love it even while one suffers,
because Life is all.
Life is God,
and to love Life means to love God."

94

*One simple act
of kindness and service*

that's in alignment with your Source

will do more to inspire others

than lectures on the virtues

of being a thoughtful citizen

ever could.

95

Truth is a necessity if you're ever going

*to live in harmony
with Spirit*

and become a source of inspiration

for the people

you encounter.

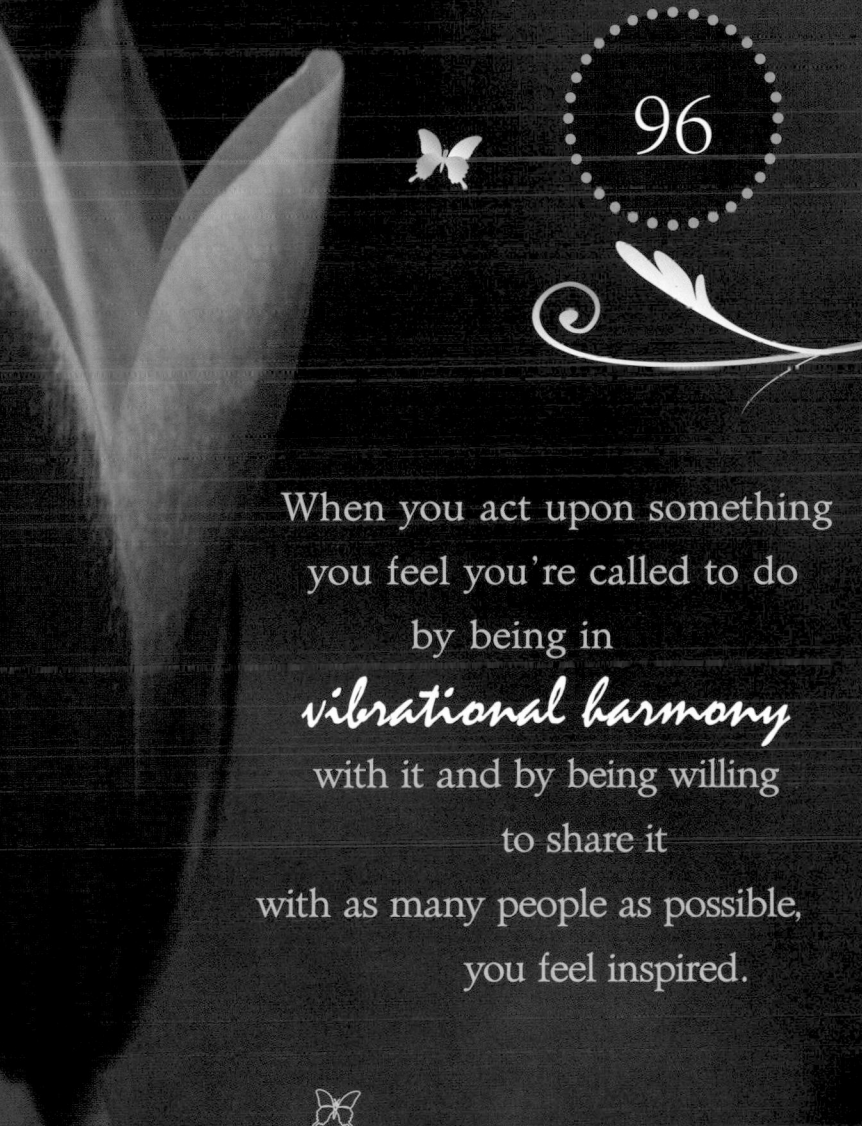

96

When you act upon something
you feel you're called to do
by being in

vibrational harmony

with it and by being willing
to share it
with as many people as possible,
you feel inspired.

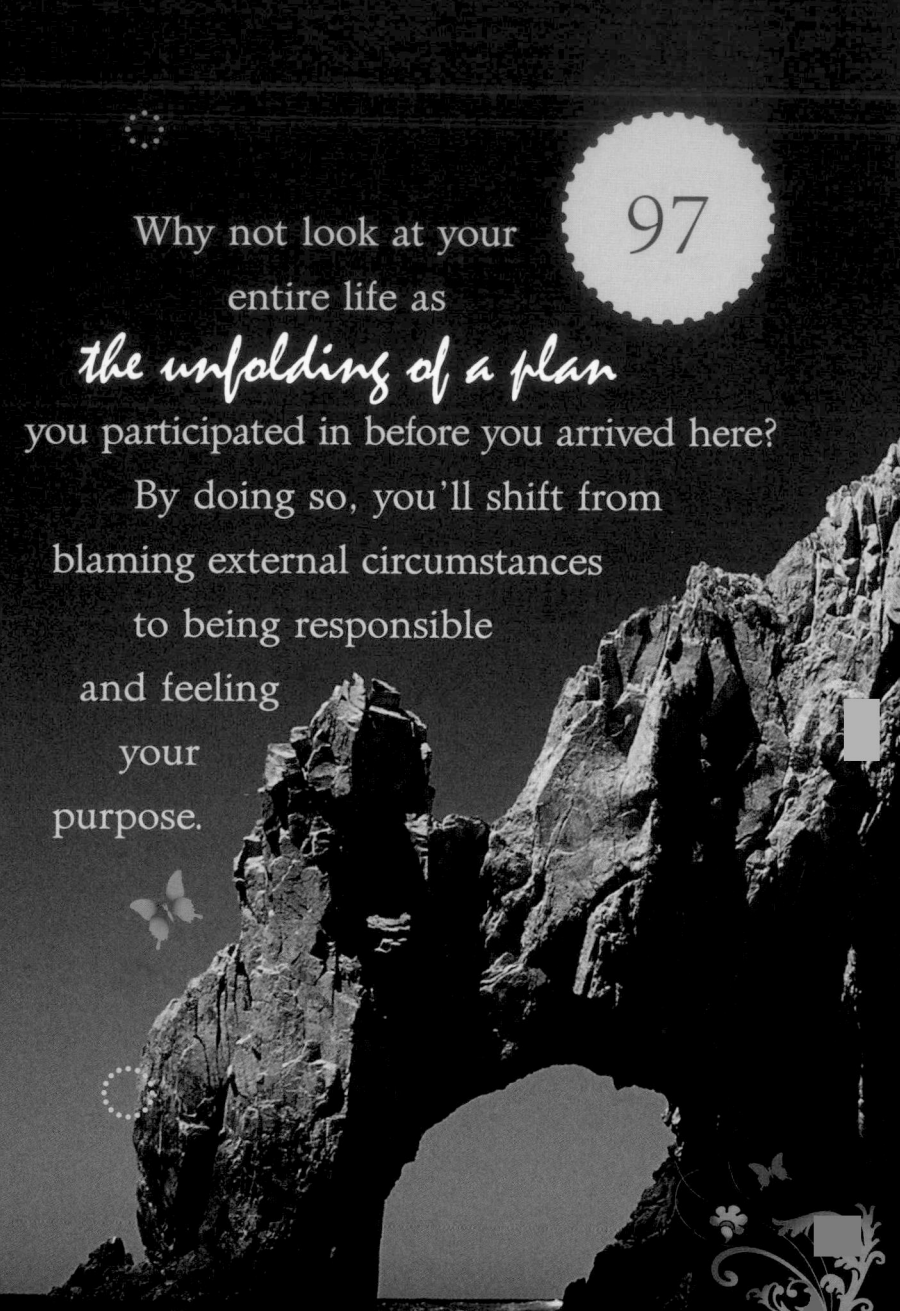

Why not look at your

97

entire life as

the unfolding of a plan

you participated in before you arrived here?
By doing so, you'll shift from
blaming external circumstances
to being responsible
and feeling
your
purpose.

98

When you take time

to meditate and commune

with Spirit,

not only will you feel revitalized,

but you'll adopt a defense system

that can't be penetrated

by efforts to uninspire you.

99

Recall that your body is a sacred temple

where you reside for this lifetime,
so make some time every single day
for exercising it.
Even if you can only
manage a walk
around the block,
just do it.

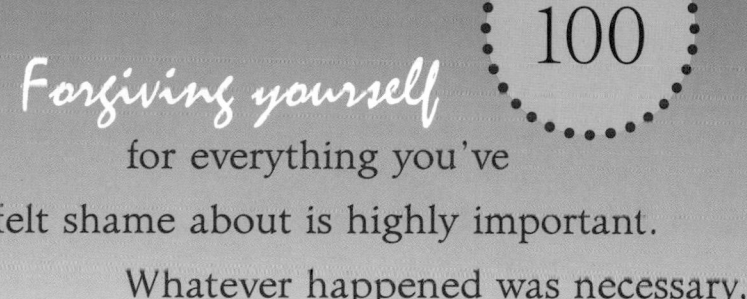

Forgiving yourself

100

for everything you've
felt shame about is highly important.
Whatever happened was necessary,
so let go of regret, and replace
your negative feelings with gratitude
for what you've learned.

101

One of Gandhi's
most illuminating observations
was that "there is more to life
than increasing its speed."
This is great advice for
simplifying your life.

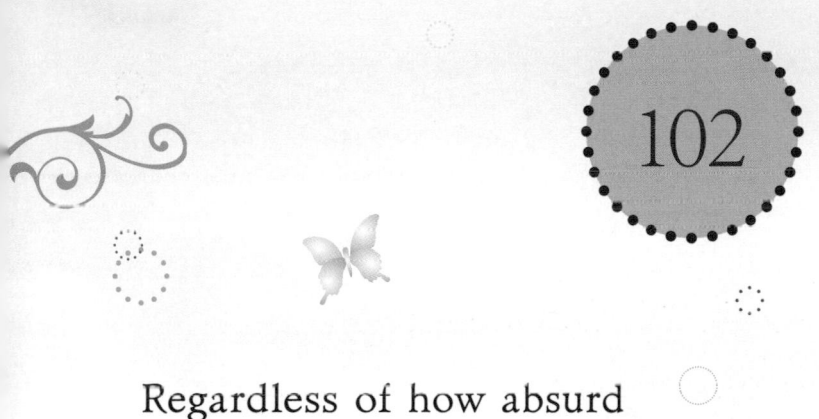

102

Regardless of how absurd
your inner callings
might seem,
they're authentically yours.
They don't have to
*make sense
to anyone else.*

103

By giving yourself free time
to read, meditate, exercise,
and walk in nature,
you're inviting the guidance
that's waiting patiently
to come calling
with inspirational
messages.

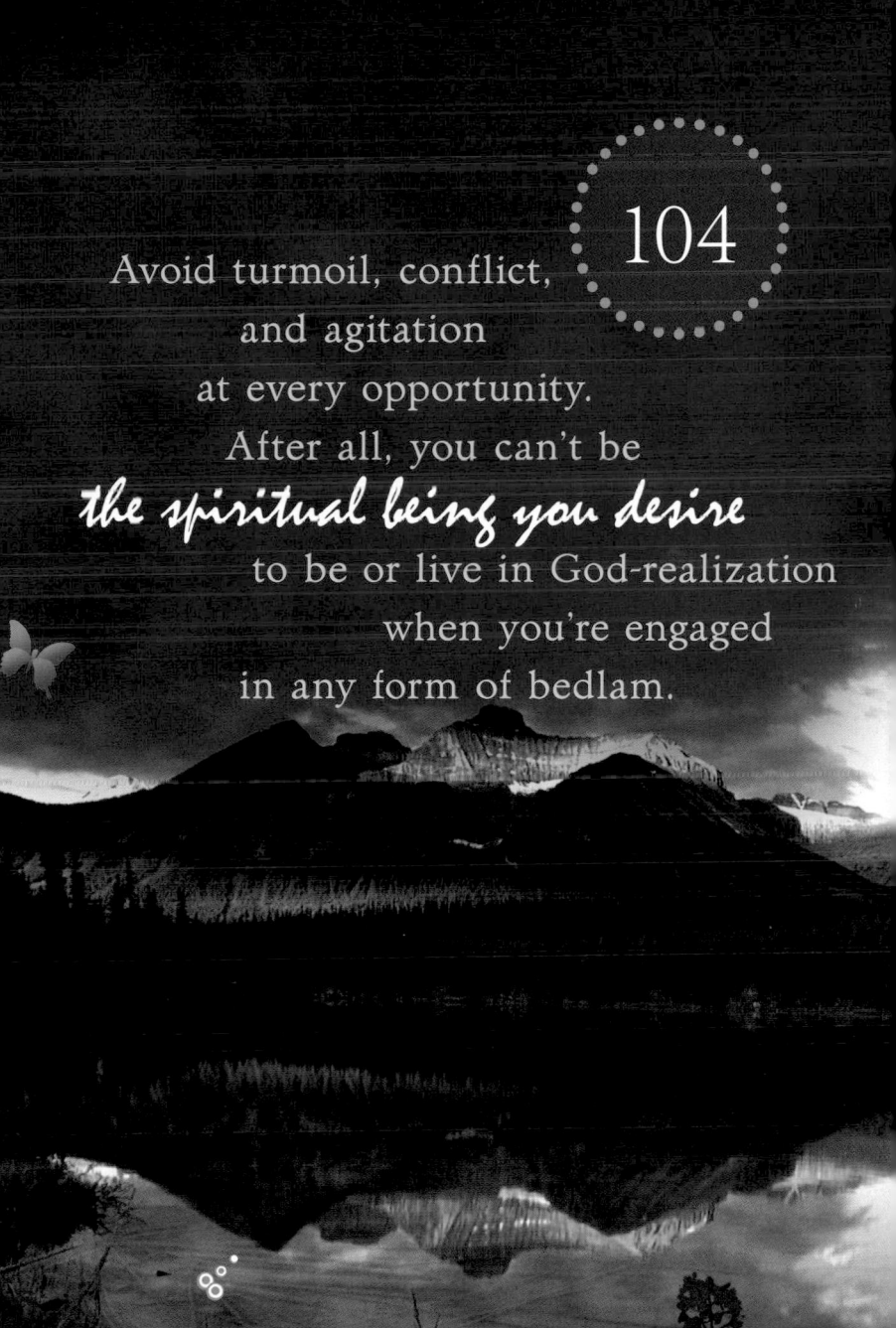

104

Avoid turmoil, conflict, and agitation at every opportunity. After all, you can't be *the spiritual being you desire* to be or live in God-realization when you're engaged in any form of bedlam.

Do everything you can to avoid debt.

Remember that *you're attempting to simplify your life,* so you don't need to purchase more of what will complicate and clutter your life. If you can't afford it, let it go until you can.

105

106

You never need to
defend yourself or your desires
to anyone,
as those inner feelings are
Spirit speaking to you.
Those thoughts are sacred,
so don't ever let anyone
trample
on them.

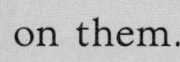

107

Source energy will cooperate with you
when you seek it energetically—
moreover, you can begin

to reassess your life

for misaligned attractions
and imagined
bad luck.

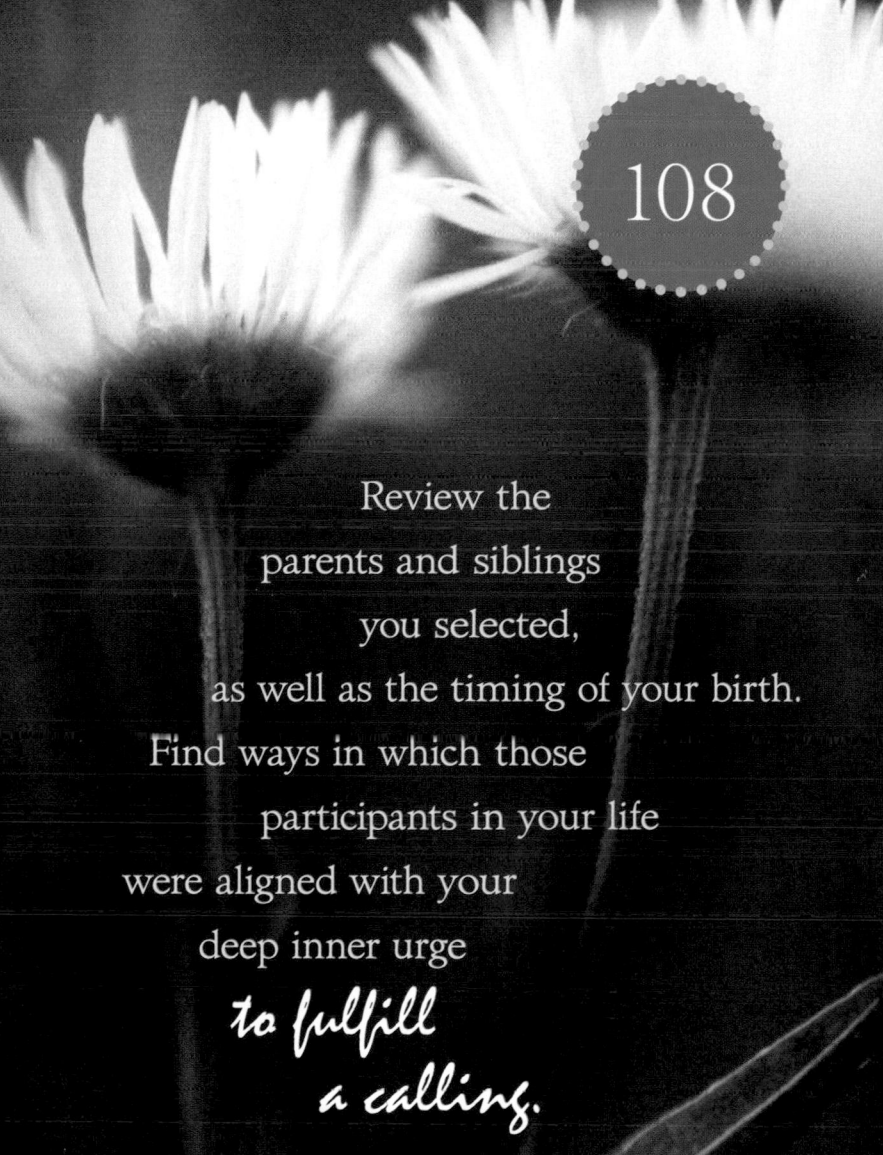

108

Review the
parents and siblings
you selected,
as well as the timing of your birth.
Find ways in which those
participants in your life
were aligned with your
deep inner urge
*to fulfill
a calling.*

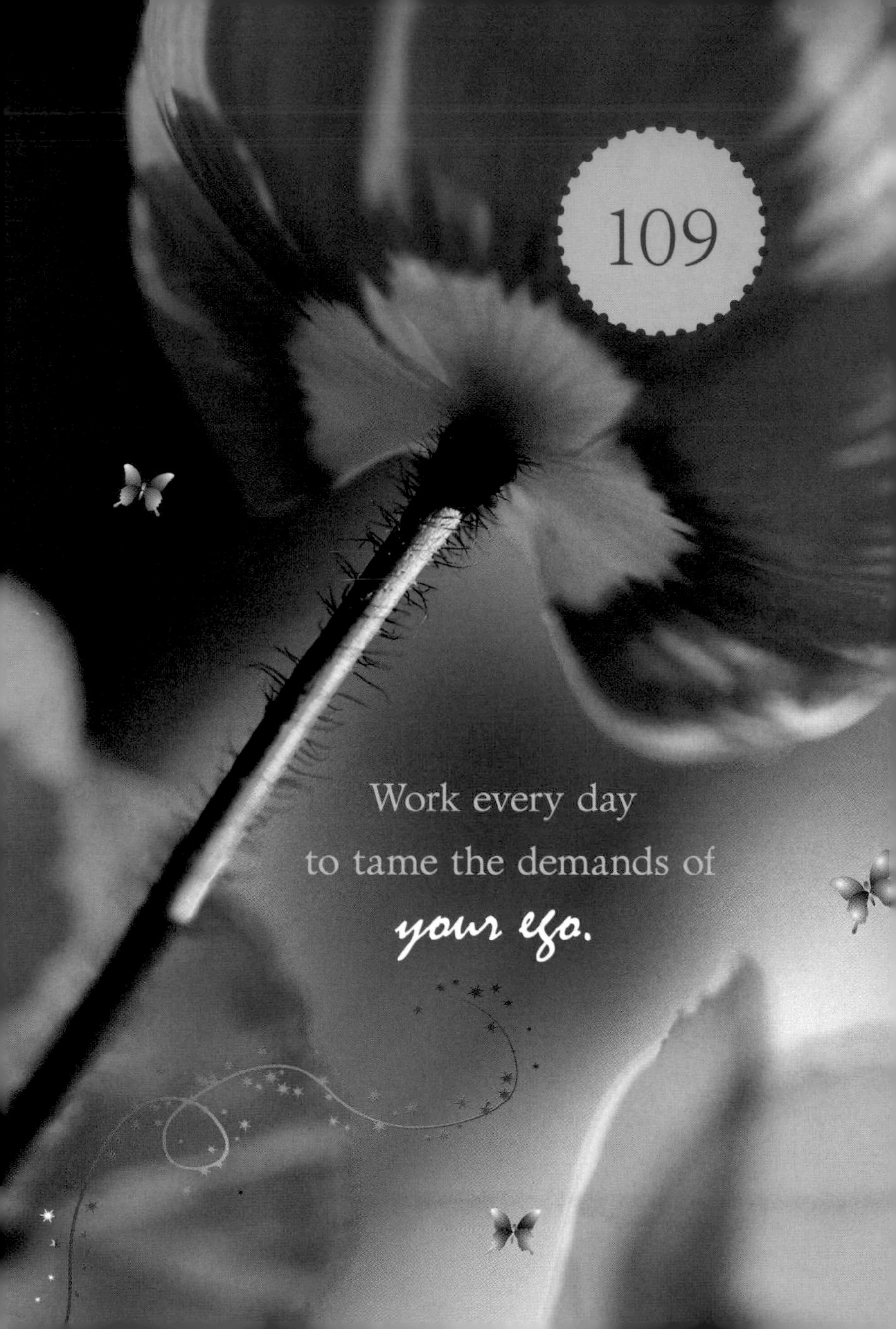

Work every day
to tame the demands of
your ego.

110

Everything in nature
is *in-Spirit*—it isn't spoiled by ego,
nor can it ever be.
So when nature speaks to you,
*you should
listen intently.*

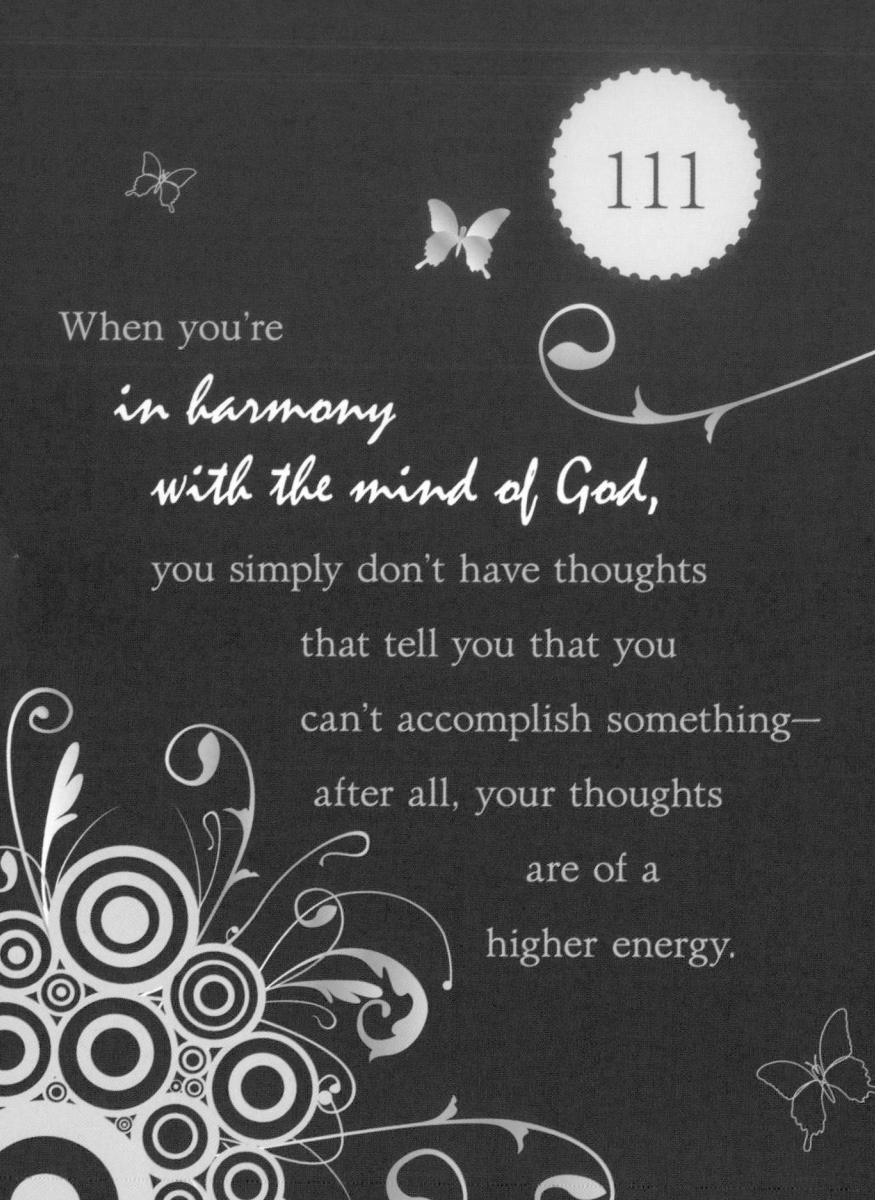

111

When you're

in harmony

with the mind of God,

you simply don't have thoughts

that tell you that you

can't accomplish something—

after all, your thoughts

are of a

higher energy.

112

*Make it a daily practice
to meditate for peace:*
yours *and* the world's.
By going within,
you make conscious
contact with your Source.

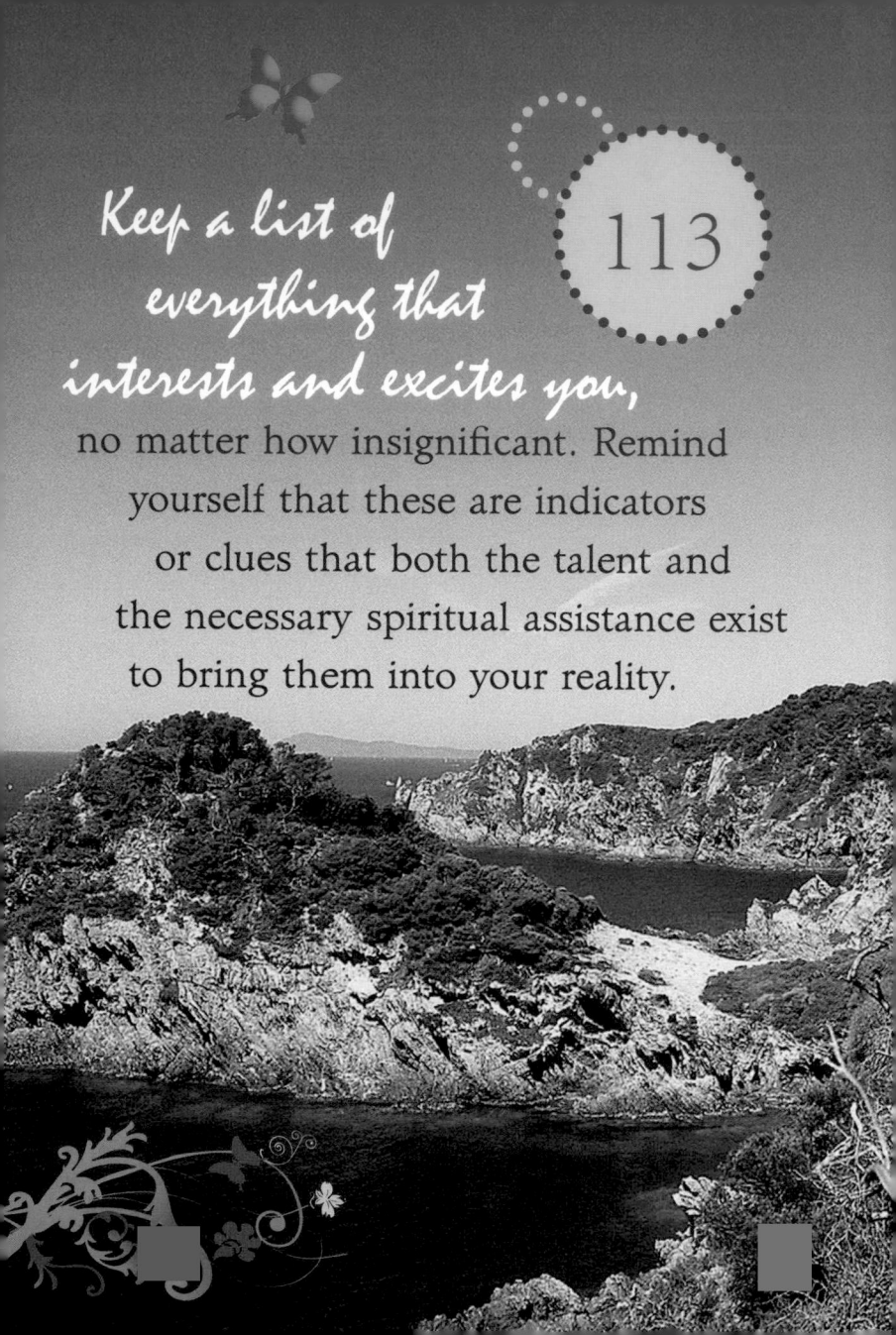

Keep a list of everything that interests and excites you,

113

no matter how insignificant. Remind yourself that these are indicators or clues that both the talent and the necessary spiritual assistance exist to bring them into your reality.

114

Returning to Spirit
results in a grand sense
of being in tune
with your
uniquely Divine purpose.

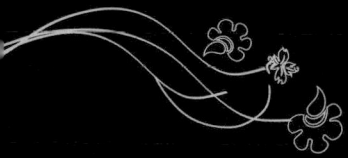

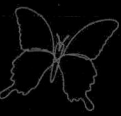

115

Your life must be open
to Spirit's guidance

in order for you to feel inspired.

So whatever it takes to feel joy,

you simply must

act upon it.

116

By choosing to live *in-Spirit*,
you entrust yourself
to something greater
than your life as
a physical being.

117

Celebrate every thought
you have,
knowing its Divine origin;
become aware of
your enormous talents;
and be awed by all that you are.

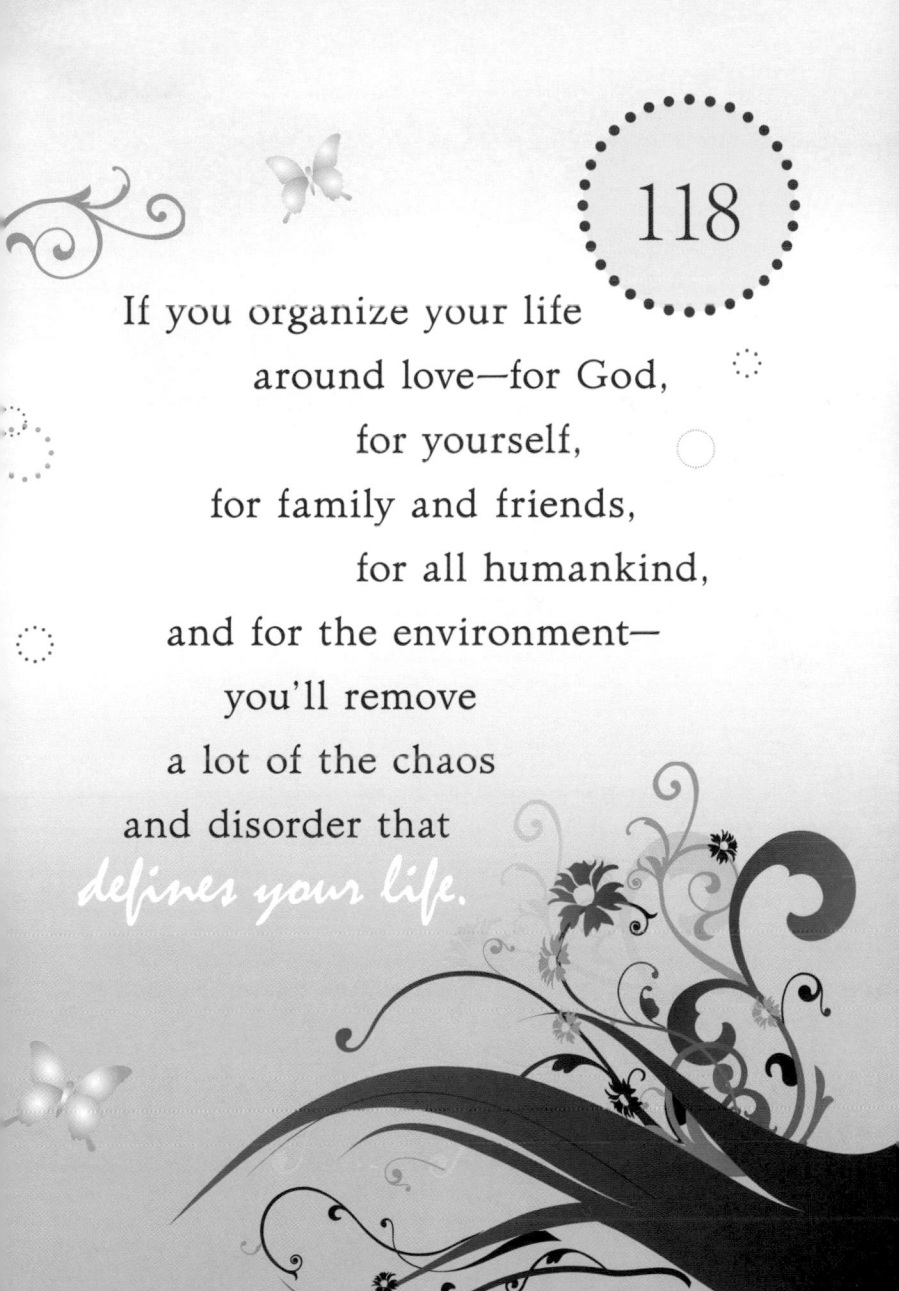

118

If you organize your life
around love—for God,
for yourself,
for family and friends,
for all humankind,
and for the environment—
you'll remove
a lot of the chaos
and disorder that
defines your life.

119

When you engage Spirit,
you regain
the power of your
ultimate Source.

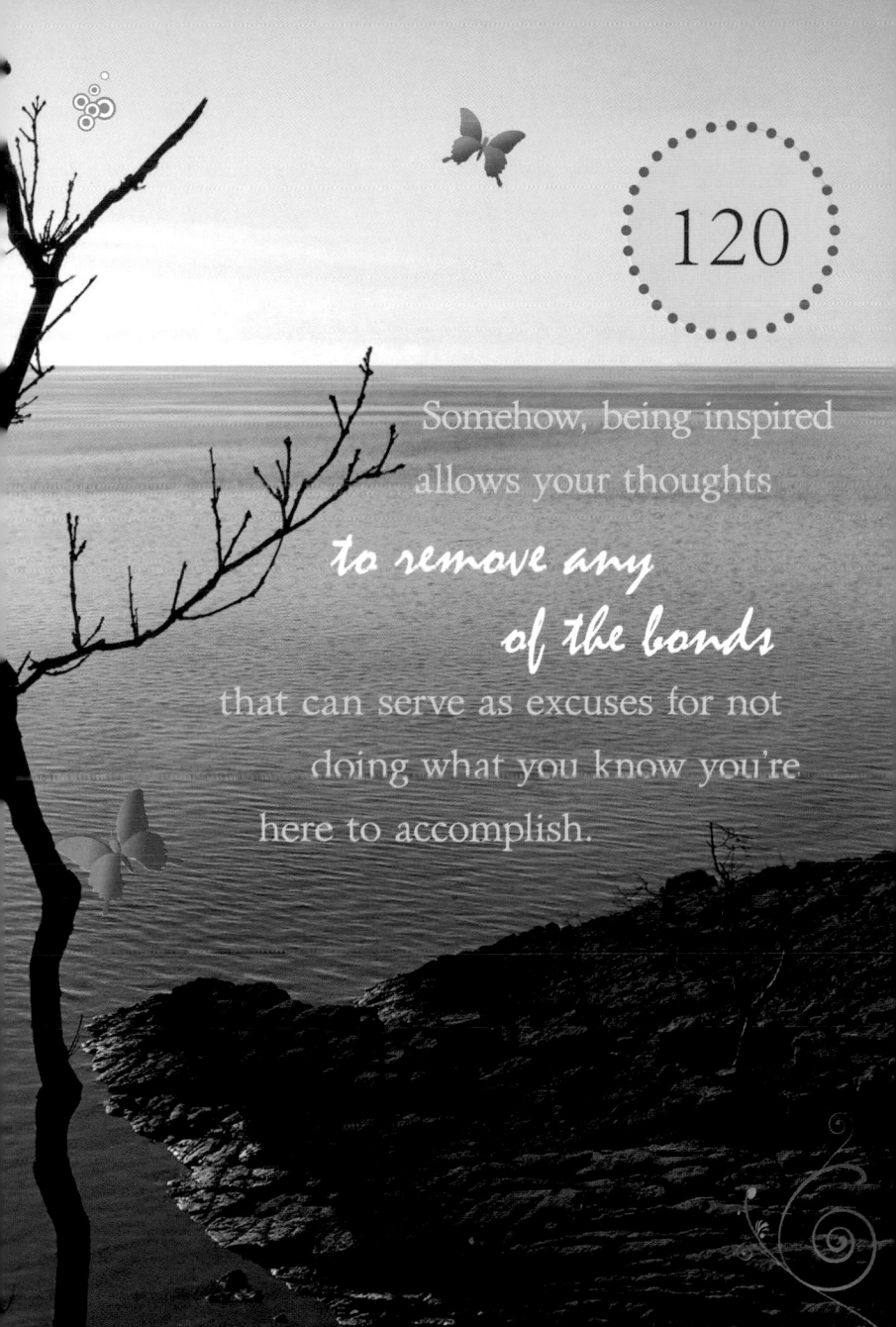

120

Somehow, being inspired
allows your thoughts
to remove any
of the bonds
that can serve as excuses for not
doing what you know you're
here to accomplish.

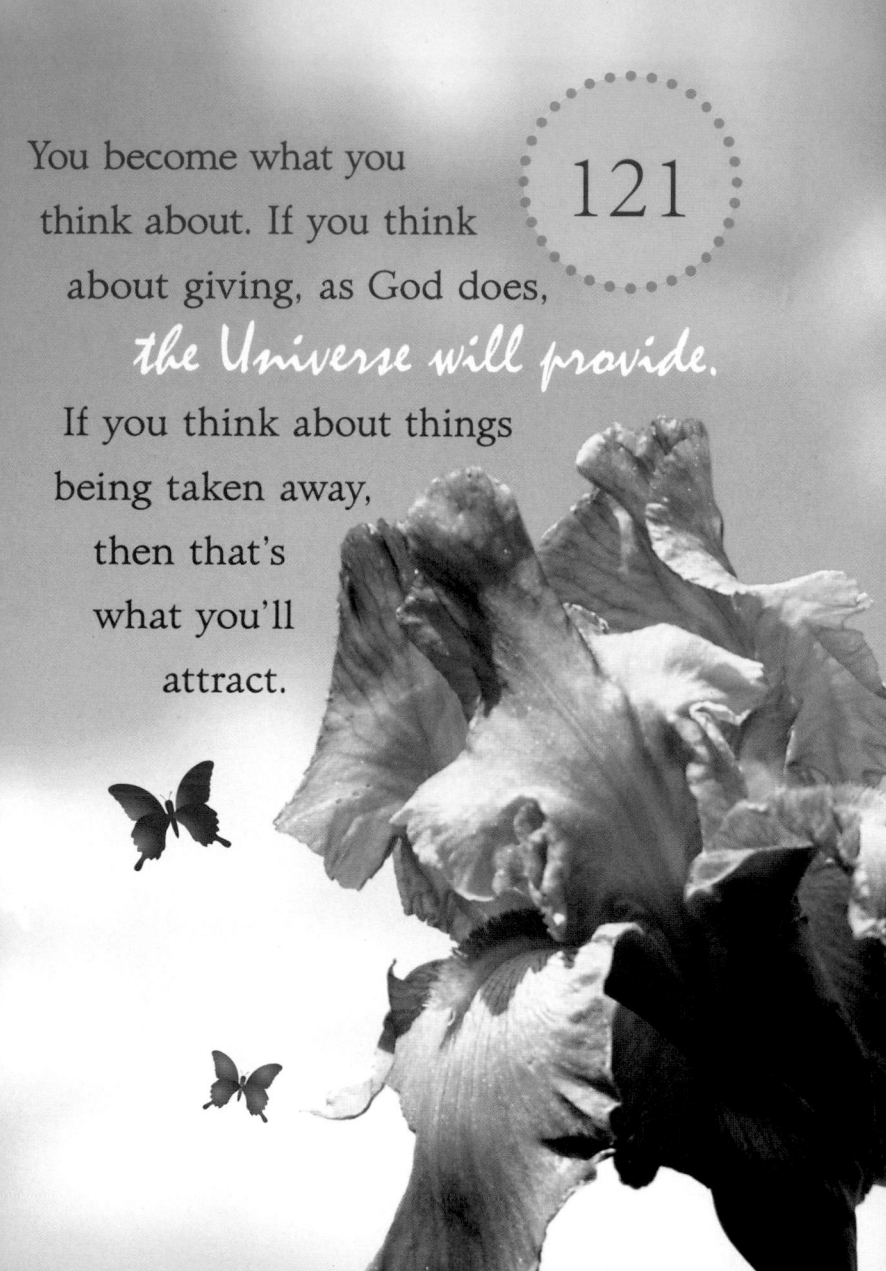

You become what you think about. If you think about giving, as God does, *the Universe will provide.* If you think about things being taken away, then that's what you'll attract.

121

122

When you're inspired,
you remember that God
*is always in you
and you're always in God,*
so you're incapable
of thinking limited thoughts.

123

Remind yourself of this truth:
If you stay in harmony
with your originating Spirit,
that invisible All-Creating Force
will go to work
on your behalf.

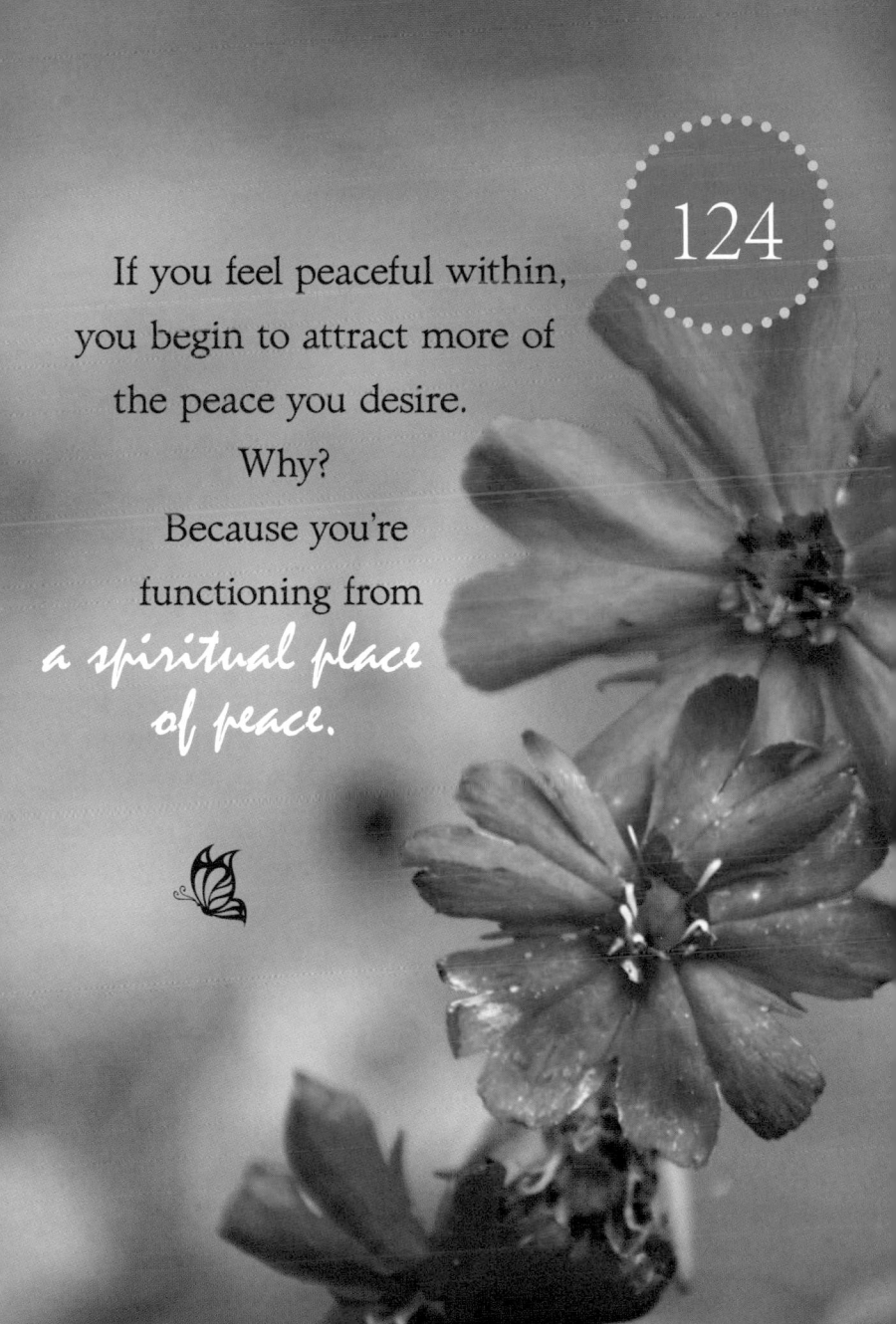

124

If you feel peaceful within,
you begin to attract more of
the peace you desire.
Why?
Because you're
functioning from
*a spiritual place
of peace.*

125

When you feel uninspired,
you recognize
that you need to make
a vibrational adjustment
that puts your thoughts and behaviors
back in alignment
with the *desire* to be inspired.

126

Remember:
You're already connected
to everything you think
is missing from your life.
All you need is a

conscious realignment

so that your thoughts begin
to match up
vibrationally with Spirit,
which you know
is a part of you already.

127

When you allow
the opinions and dictates
of others
to determine what you're going to be,
you lose sight
of your objective to live an inspired life.

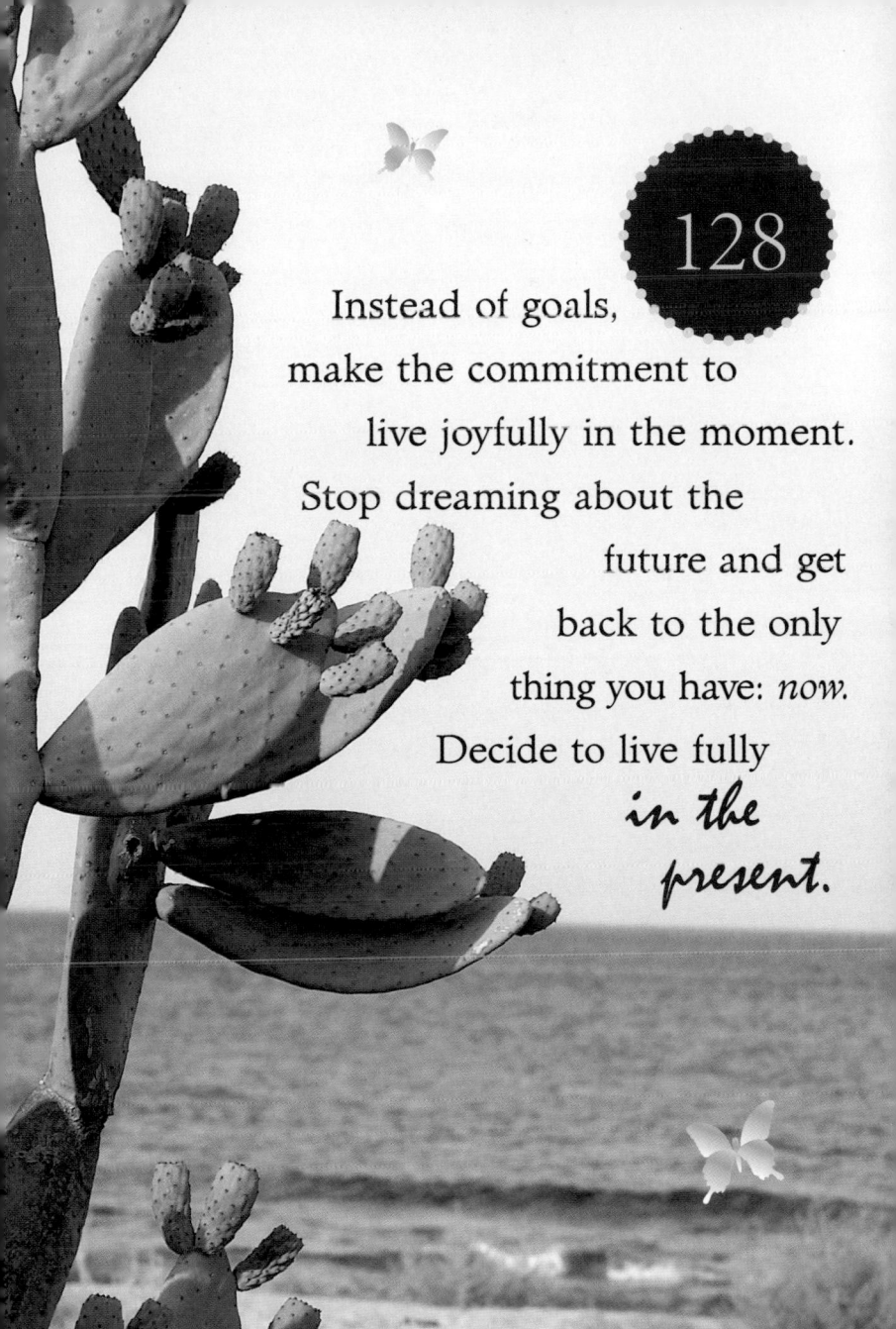

128

Instead of goals,
make the commitment to
live joyfully in the moment.
Stop dreaming about the
future and get
back to the only
thing you have: *now*.
Decide to live fully
*in the
present.*

129

The fundamental truth that
*you need to recite
and know is:*

*I am a Divine creation.
All creation has purpose.
I am here to be
like God!*

130

Anything that's
causing excitement within you
is evidence of a
message from Spirit
that's saying,
"You can do this—yes, you can!"

131

Your physical presence
is made up of the same stuff
that makes up the stars.
That's right, the stuff of dreams—
twinkling, magical,
beautiful,
light-filled stardust!

132

When you immerse yourself
in movies, television shows,
plays, and recordings
tendered by
individuals and organizations
that reflect a rapport
with Spirit,
you increase your

daily inspiration level.

133

Maintain the awareness
of your blessed, Divine, perfect body
that's capable of anything
you desire.

134

Read biographies of people who
reflect your ideas of
high spiritual energy,
be they historical
or contemporary figures.
Just by spending time
reading about their lives,
you'll feel a great sense
of inspiration.

135

Be leery of invitations
to functions that may keep you on
top of society's pyramid,
but which inhibit your access
to joyful inspiration.
Begin declining
invitations
that don't activate
feelings
of inspiration.

136

As you
practice speaking
from your truth
without being hurtful
or arrogant in any way,
*you reconnect with
the energy*
you emanated from
in the first place.

137

When life tends to get
overly complex, too fast,
too cluttered,
too deadline oriented,
or too type A for you,
*stop and remember
your own spirit.*

You don't have to *endure criticism* with anything other than a polite thank-you and a promise to consider what's been said—anything else is a state of conflict that erases the possibility of your feeling inspired.

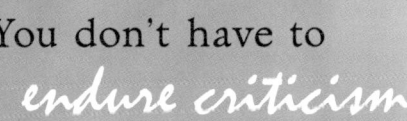

138

139

Your alternative
to feeling down
when you're exposed to
a media offense of bad news
is to instantly remind yourself
that you refuse to be
a vibrational match
to anything
uninspiring.

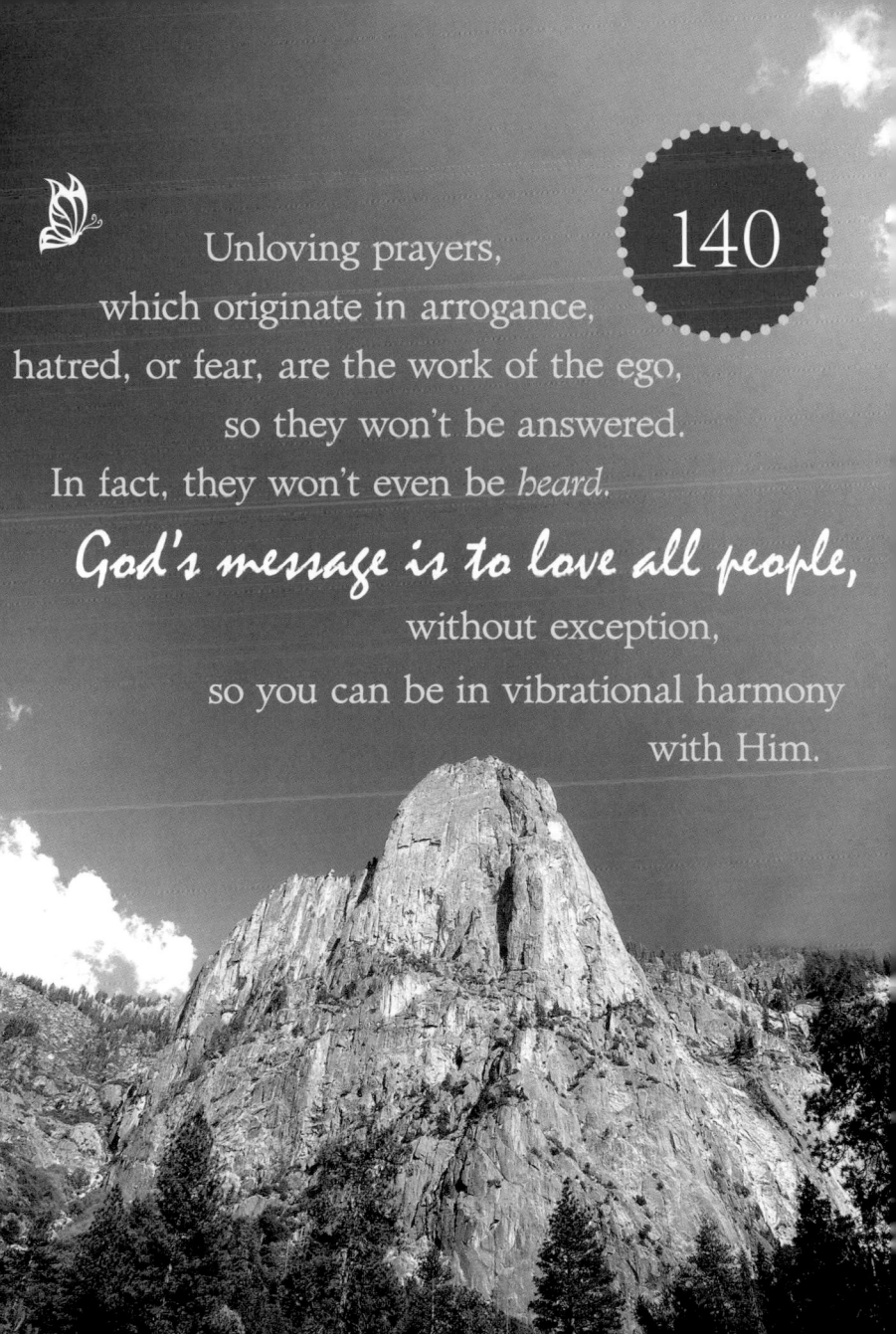

140

Unloving prayers,
which originate in arrogance,
hatred, or fear, are the work of the ego,
so they won't be answered.
In fact, they won't even be *heard*.

God's message is to love all people,
without exception,
so you can be in vibrational harmony
with Him.

141

You'll simplify your life and feel inspired
if you learn to *play*,
rather than work,
your way through life.

142

Think about some
of the most inspirational people
in your life
and tell them precisely
why you admire them.
As you express your appreciation,
you'll feel inspired
by this simple act of
acknowledgment.

143

When you're at peace
with your life and
in a state of
tranquility, you actually send out
a vibration of energy
that impacts all living creatures,
including plants, animals . . .
and even babies!

144

The answers
to the resolution
of poverty and scarcity
are readily available to you,
and they'd be resolved tomorrow
if you remembered that
we're all *one* on this planet:
We all share the same origins,
and we all end up
back in the same nonplace
where we began.

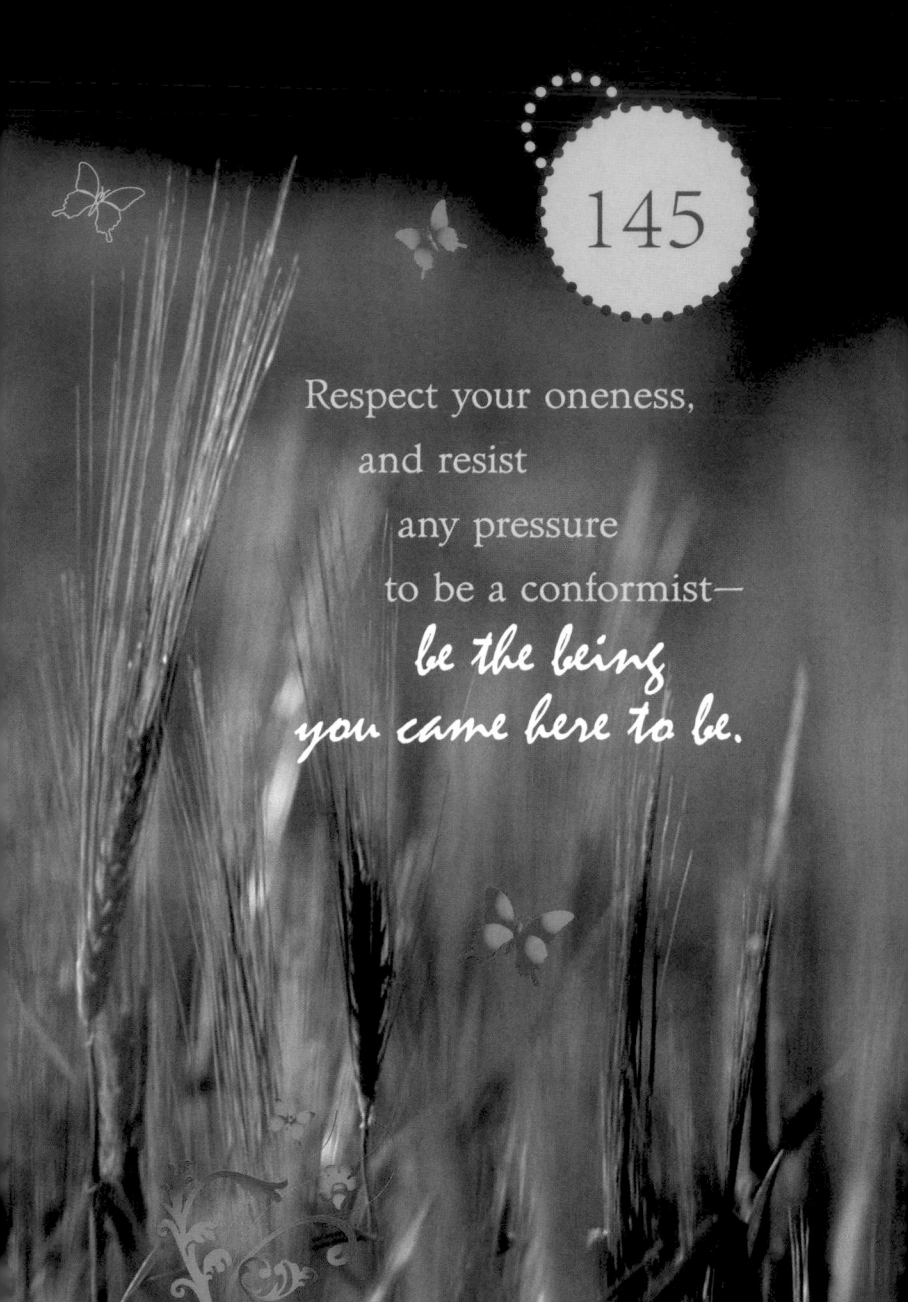

145

Respect your oneness,
and resist
any pressure
to be a conformist—
*be the being
you came here to be.*

146

Be a good listener.

It makes the person

who's speaking to you

feel loved, cared for,

and worthy of being heard.

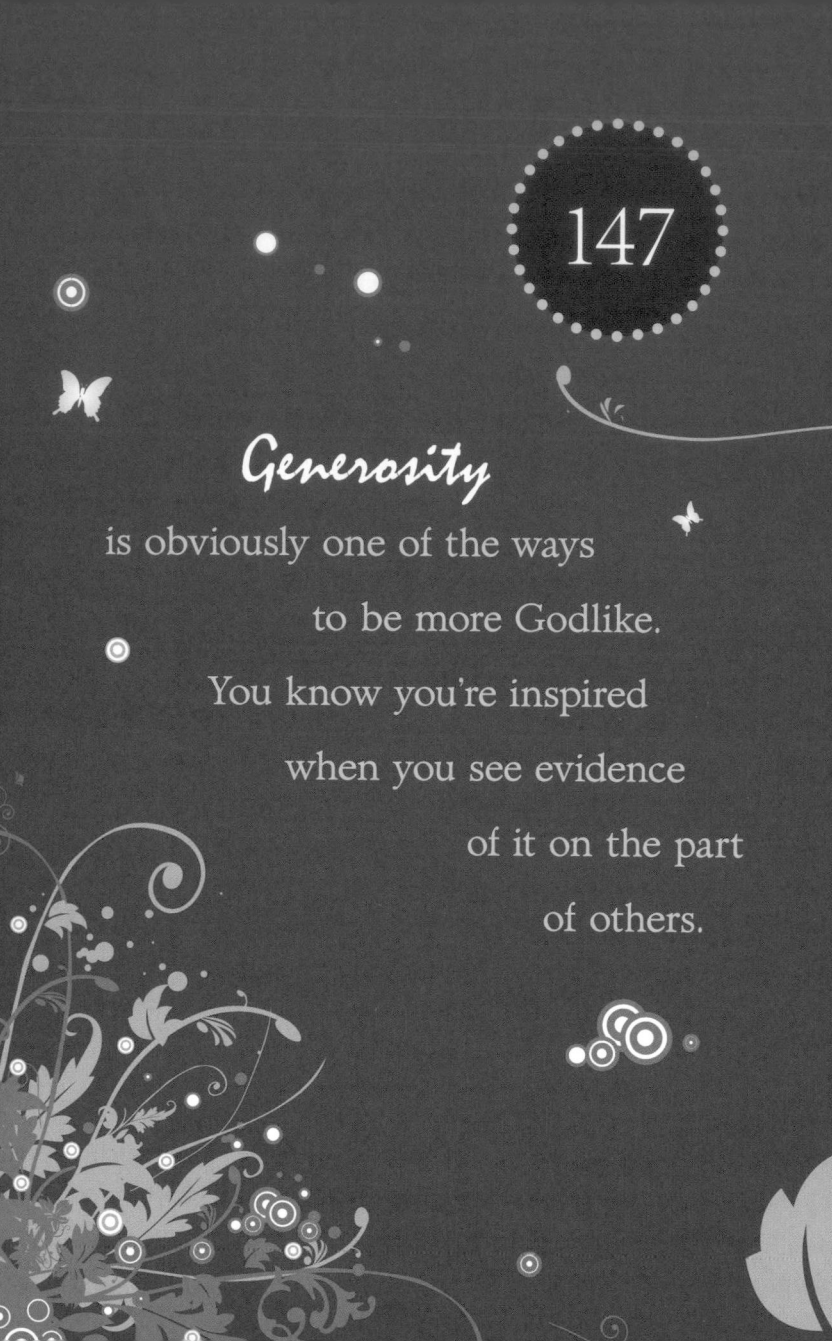

147

Generosity

is obviously one of the ways

to be more Godlike.

You know you're inspired

when you see evidence

of it on the part

of others.

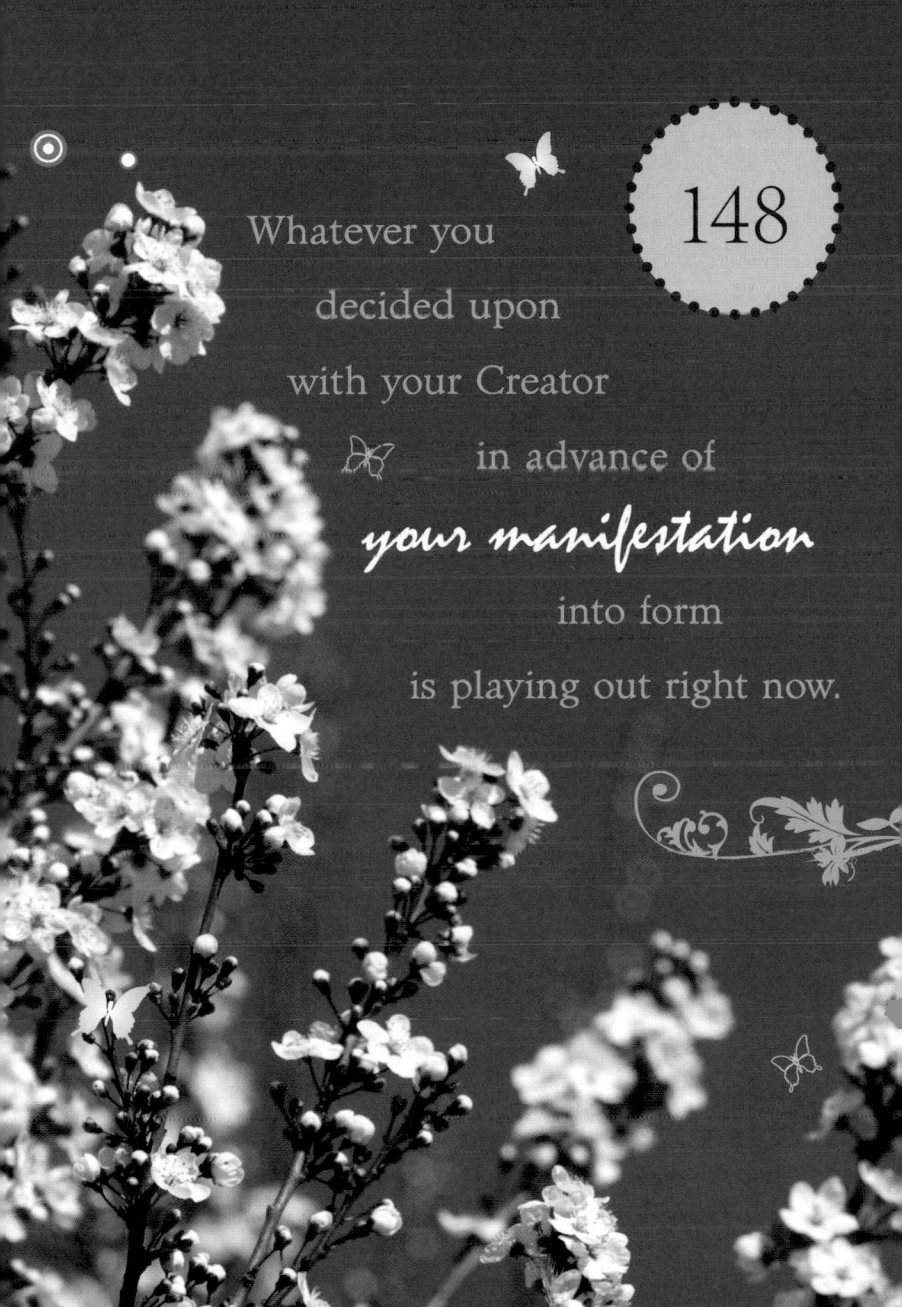

148

Whatever you

decided upon

with your Creator

in advance of

your manifestation

into form

is playing out right now.

149

Practice daily meditation

to become more peaceful,

and then watch as others
who previously engaged
you in confrontation
are less inclined in that direction.

150

When you banish all doubt

in favor of faith,

there's nothing

more powerful

on this planet.

151

If your desire is to

attract wealth and prosperity,

then you must entertain

prosperous thoughts

that match your desire

and that activate

the manifestation

process.

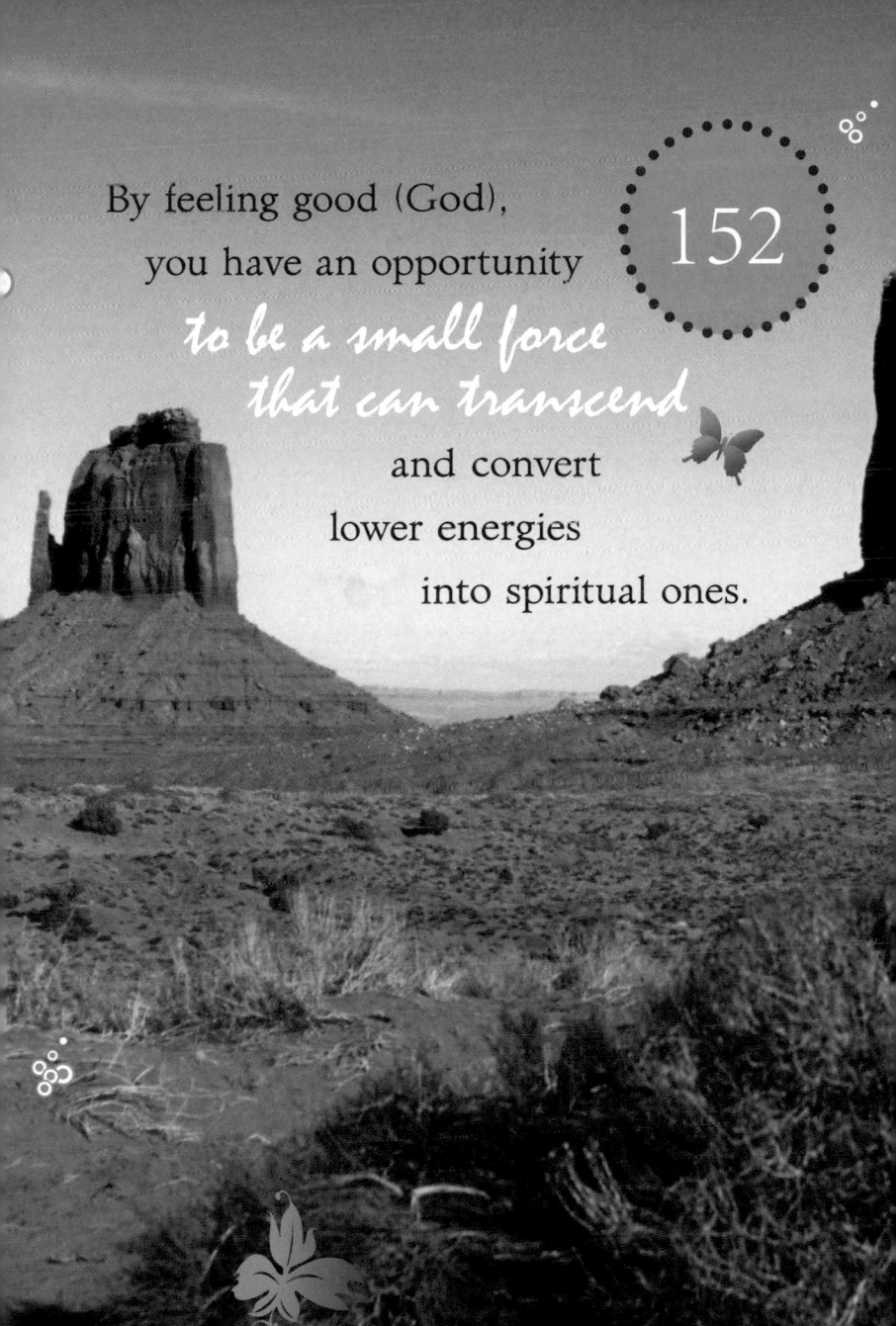

By feeling good (God),
you have an opportunity
*to be a small force
that can transcend*
and convert
lower energies
into spiritual ones.

152

153

Upon awakening,

decide

to do something—anything—

that will improve

the quality of life

for someone,

without seeking

any credit for yourself.

154

Just as the
Prayer of St. Francis
reminds you that
it is in giving that you receive,
in order to receive inspiration
*you must be willing
to give it away,*
and vice versa.

155

Remember that your body/mind

is the greatest pharmacy ever created.

*It has an unlimited potential
for creating well-being,*

since that's where

it originated from

in the first place!

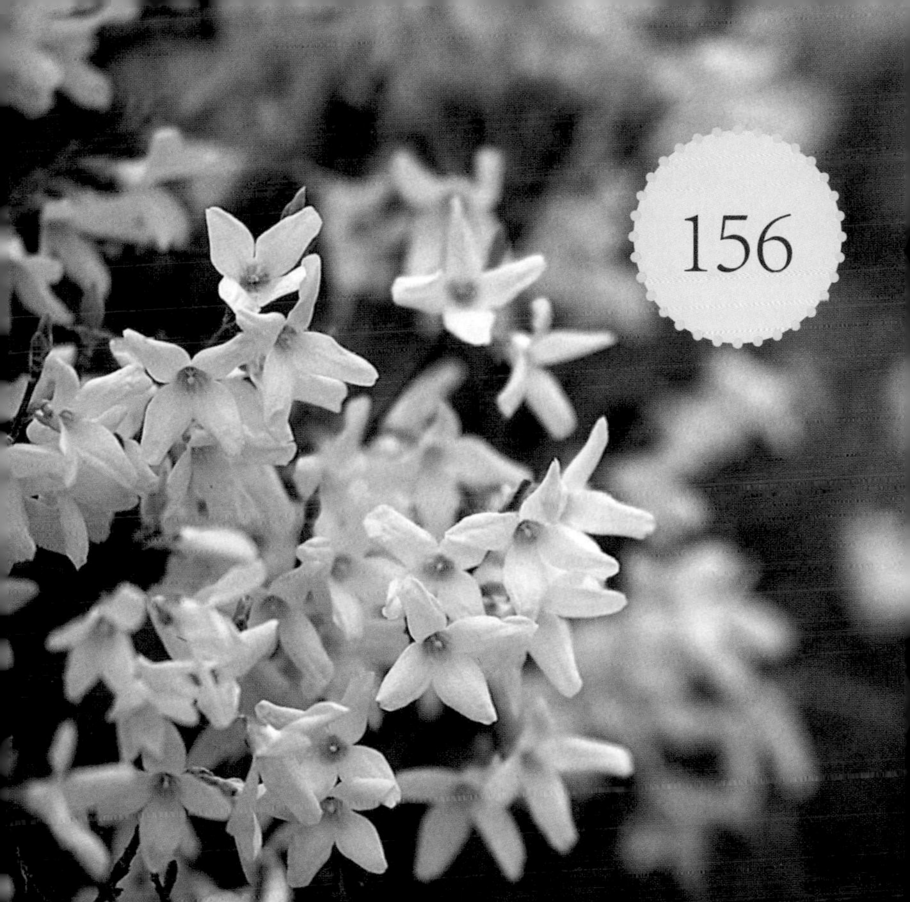

156

Keep in mind that you can't co-create with anyone, including your Spiritual Source, unless you're *in a place of harmony.*

You don't have to learn
a single new thing in order to

*communicate and
make conscious
contact*

with your Source—
it's all in you already.

158

Even though
you're on loan
for this temporary human experience,
you're never,
ever forgotten by God,
the Source that provides you
and everything else that
lives and breathes
with the energy
to sustain life.

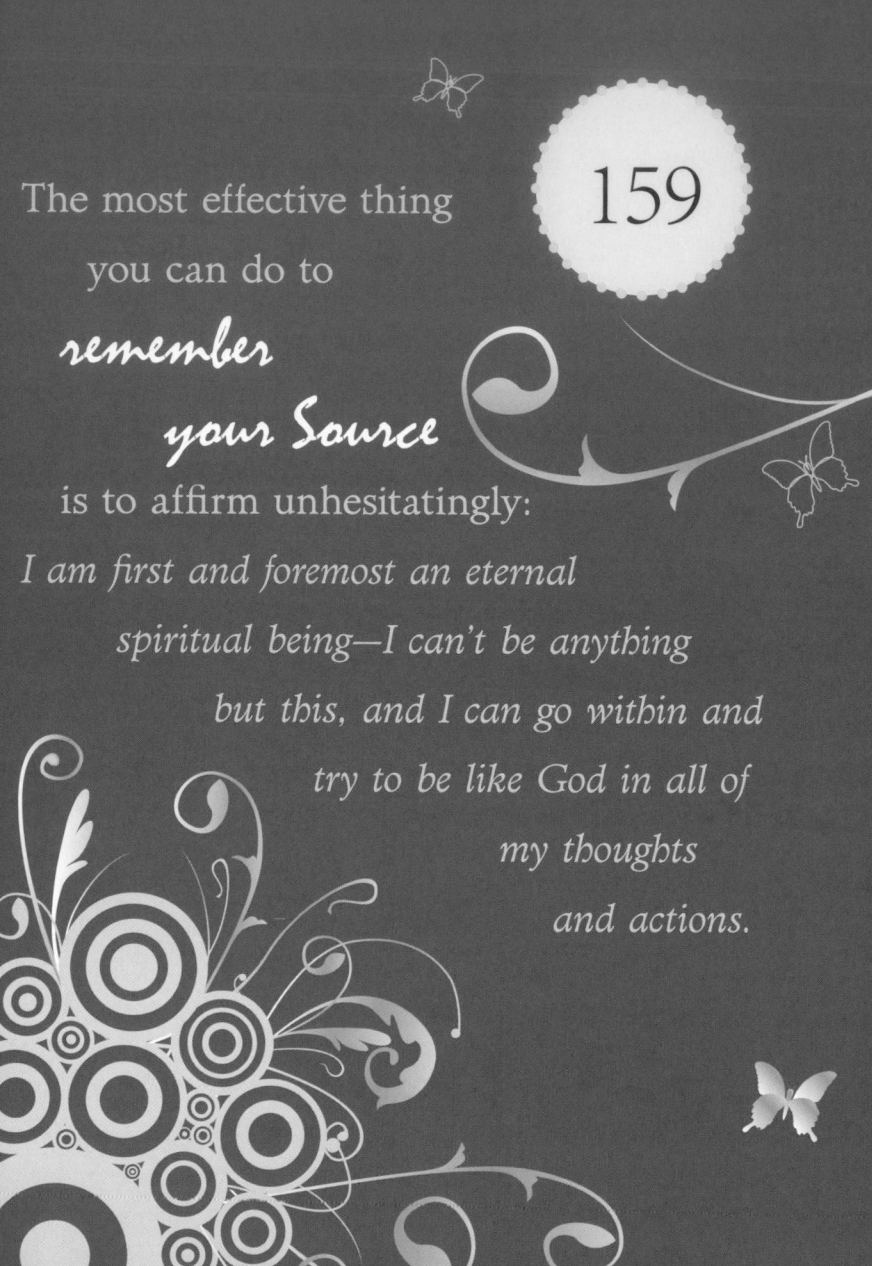

The most effective thing
you can do to

remember

your Source

is to affirm unhesitatingly:
I am first and foremost an eternal

spiritual being—I can't be anything

but this, and I can go within and

try to be like God in all of

my thoughts

and actions.

159

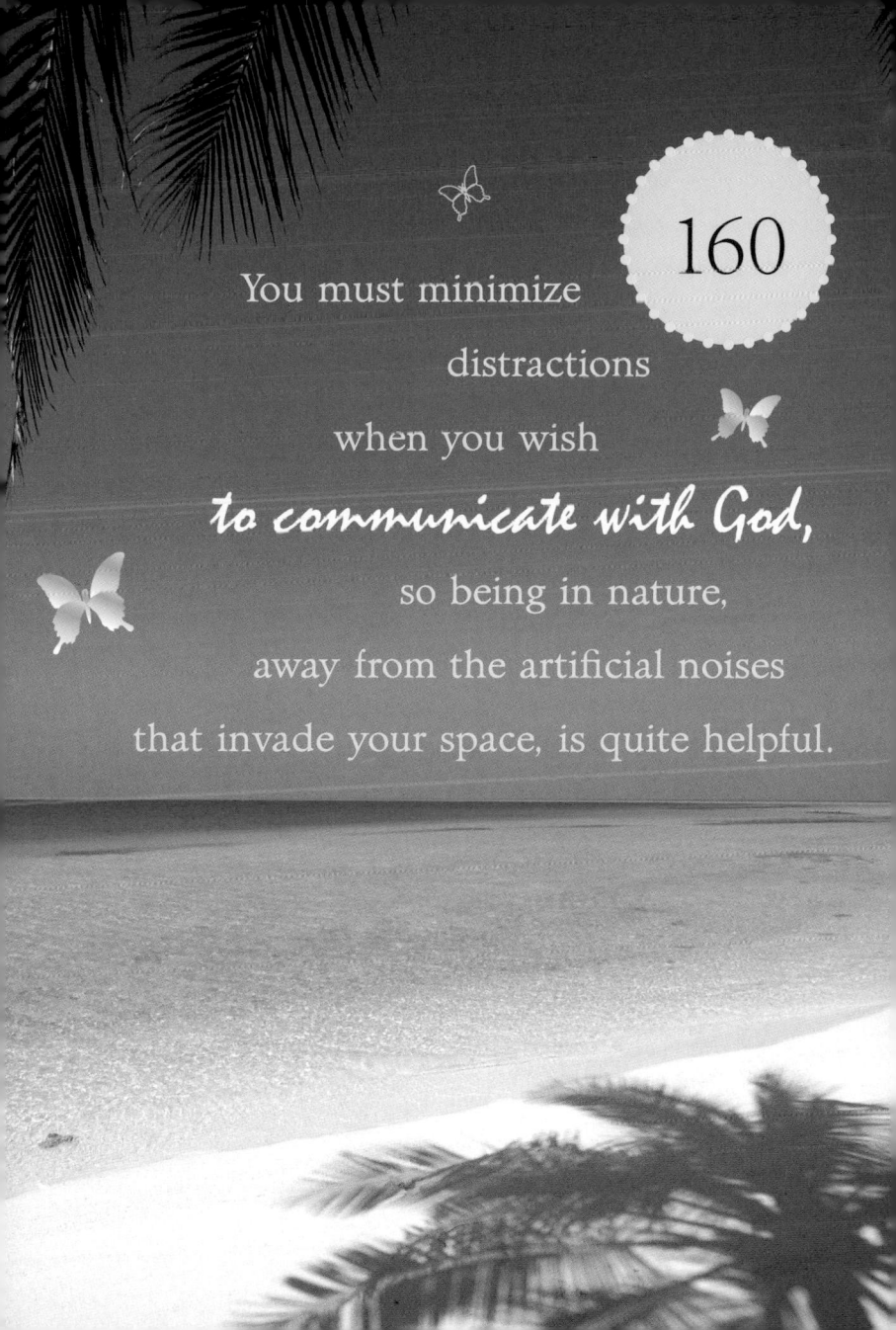

160

You must minimize
distractions
when you wish
to communicate with God,
so being in nature,
away from the artificial noises
that invade your space, is quite helpful.

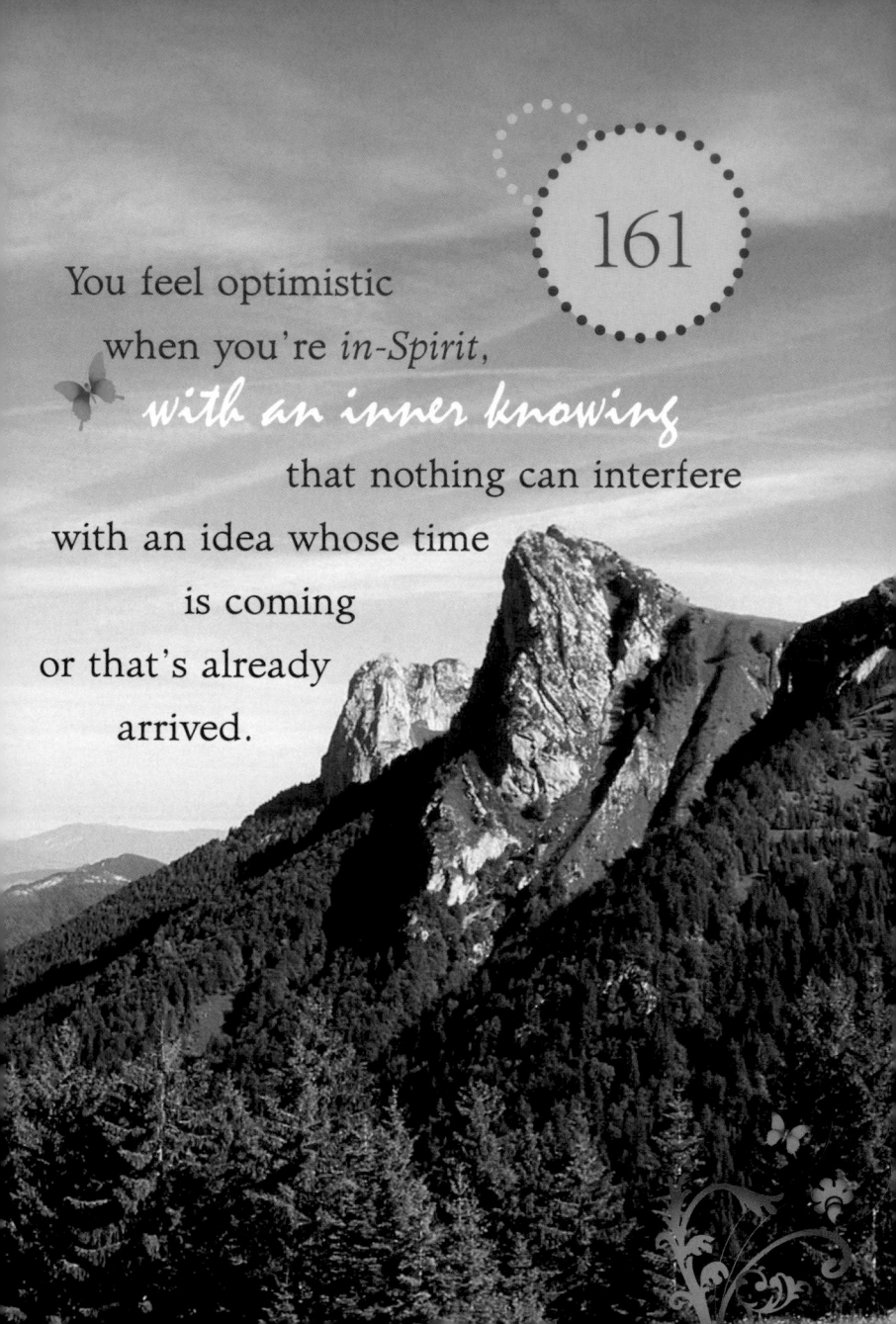

161

You feel optimistic
when you're *in-Spirit*,
with an inner knowing
that nothing can interfere
with an idea whose time
is coming
or that's already
arrived.

162

When you feel inspired,

*you notice how much zest
you have for life*

and everything that you do,

whether it's playing tennis,

helping your kids with their homework,

or doing chores around the house.

163

As a result of being
more and more inspired,
you see Spirit
in virtually everyone
you meet.

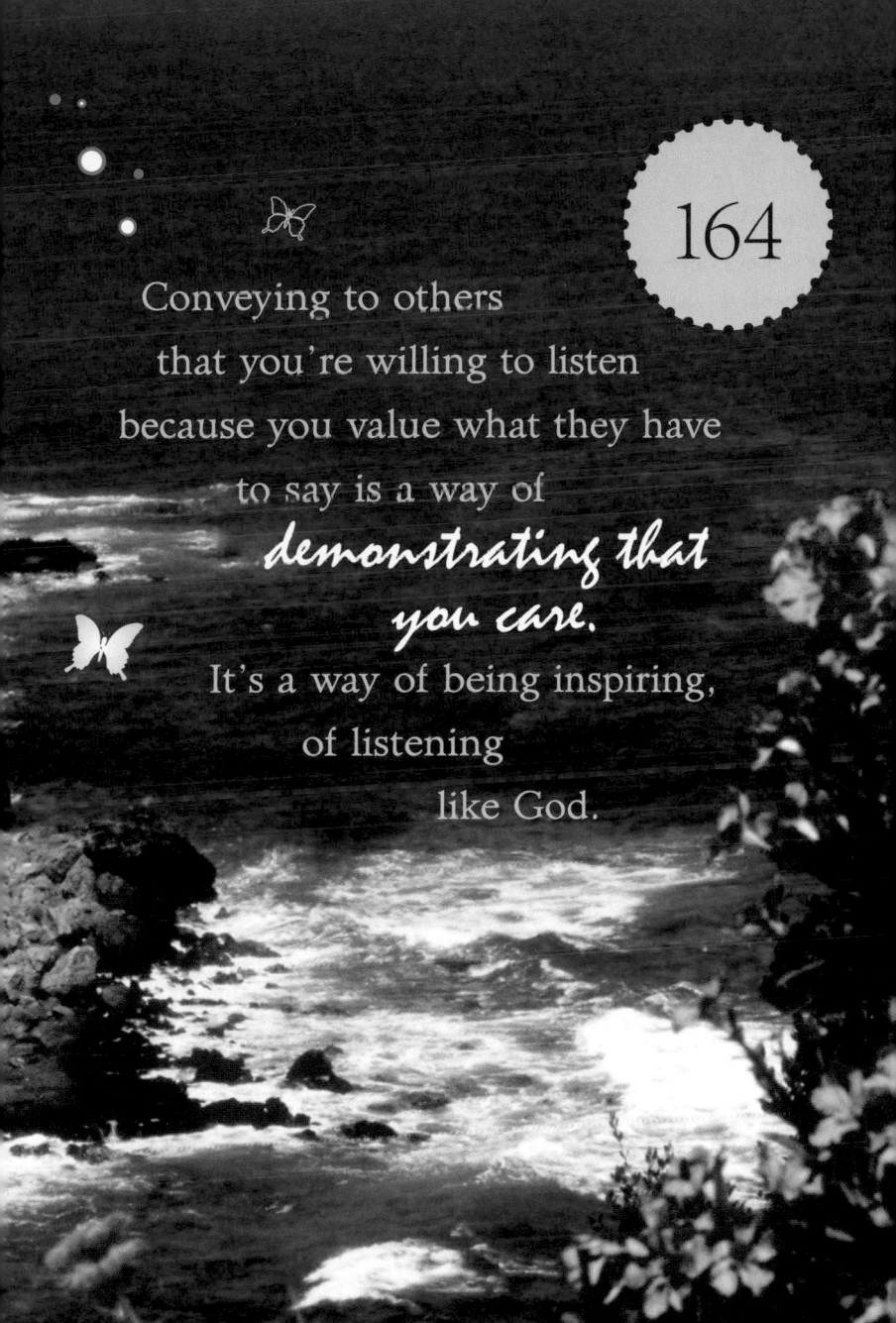

164

Conveying to others
that you're willing to listen
because you value what they have
to say is a way of
*demonstrating that
you care.*
It's a way of being inspiring,
of listening
like God.

165

The language of Spirit will often proclaim
its creativity by producing sequences
of repetition *to align you with
your Source*. In other words,
such occurrences are not accidents—
your teachers are not only
showing up, they're
practically hitting you
over the head!

166

Being inspired

is an experience of joy:

You feel completely connected

to your Source

and totally on purpose,

your creative juices flow,

and you bring

exceptionally high energy

to your daily life.

167

My life is bigger than I am.
Remind yourself
of this statement.
Print it out
and post it strategically
in your
home, car,
or workplace.

168

When you have thoughts
that reflect hatred,
judgment,
and exclusion,

be aware

that you're moving away
from your Source.

169

There are no accidents

in a Universe directed
by a Source energy that creates
endless real magic in the
form of its creations.

Throughout various stages of
life, inspiration is the
thought or idea *reconnecting you
to the energy* you were part of
prior to becoming a microscopic
particle. This is called
"surrendering to your destiny and
allowing yourself to hear
the call."

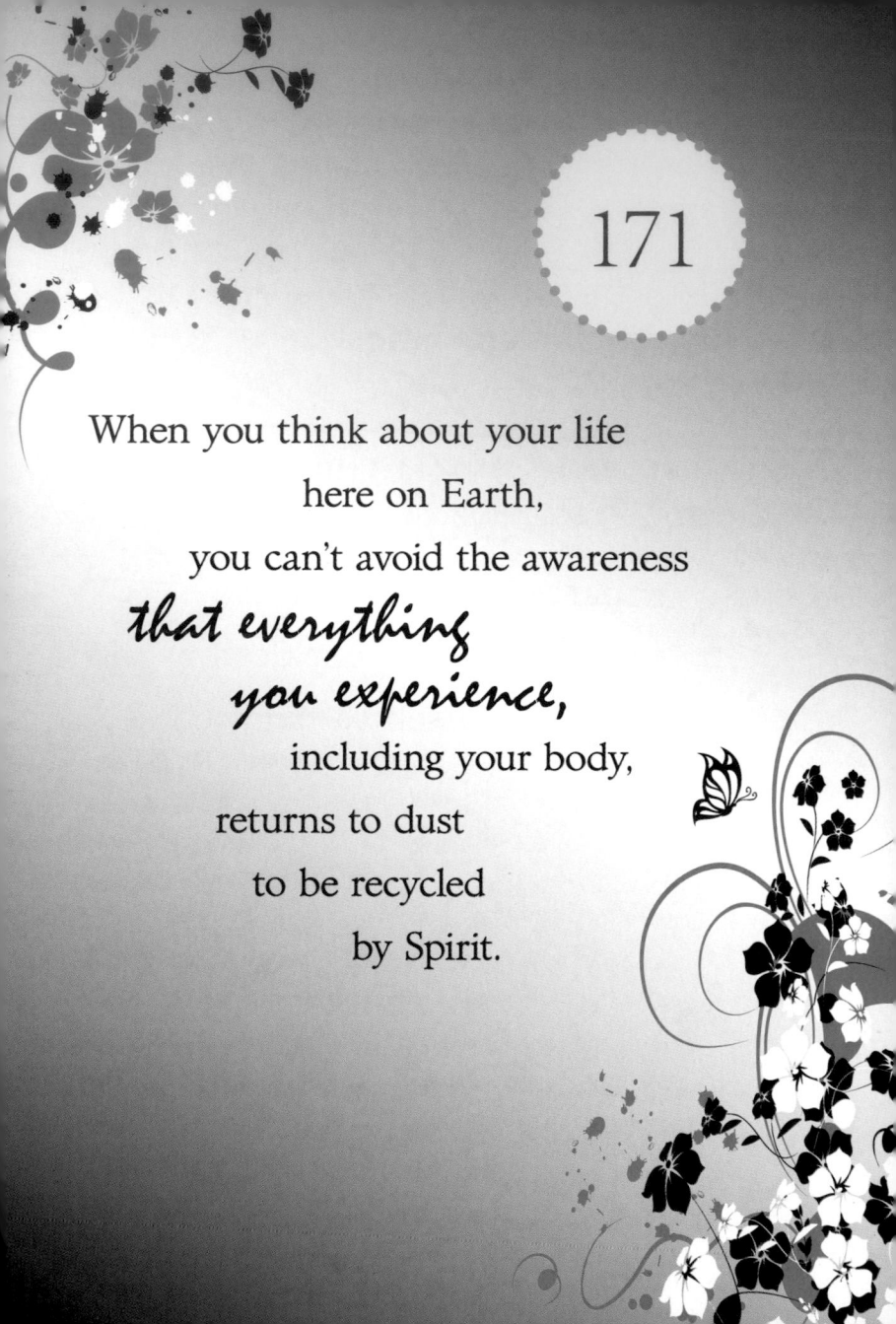

171

When you think about your life
here on Earth,
you can't avoid the awareness
*that everything
you experience,*
including your body,
returns to dust
to be recycled
by Spirit.

Any energy you place
on what transpired in the past
is groundwork for guilt,
and ego loves guilt.
Such negative energy
fabricates an excuse
for why your present moments
are troubled
and gives you a cop-out,
a reason to stay out of Spirit.

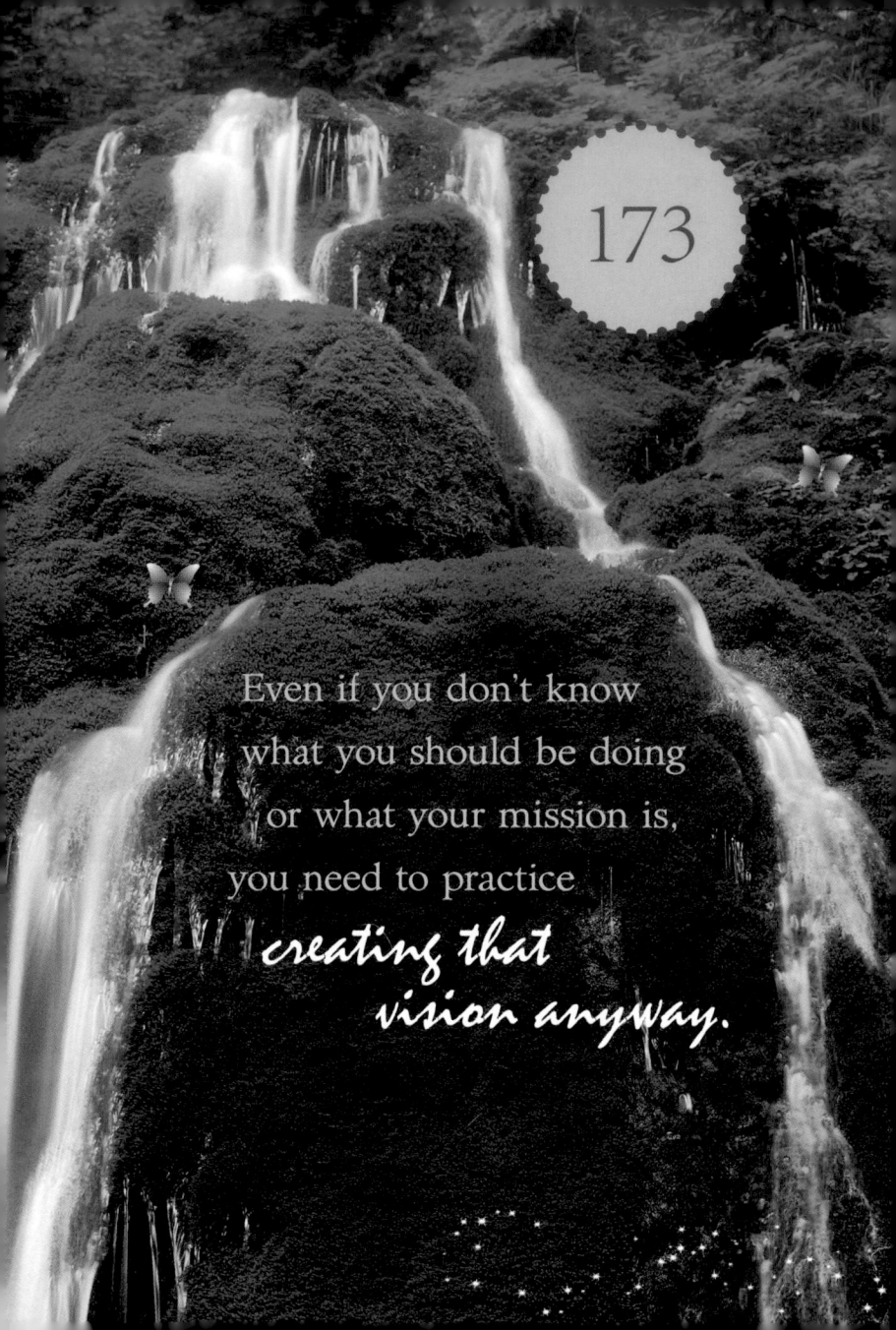

173

Even if you don't know
what you should be doing
or what your mission is,
you need to practice

*creating that
vision anyway.*

174

When you're inspired,
you attract abundance
from that which you originated.
And the mind then
truly transcends
every limitation.

175

The journey
to feeling purposeful
and inspired
*begins by seeking
to be like God*
in all of your thoughts
and actions.

Even in devastating natural disasters such as hurricanes, tsunamis, floods, fires, and the like, *look for the good.* There's no death from the perspective of infinity, so once you've removed the horror of dying from the equation, you'll have a different perspective.

177

*When you contemplate
your Creator,*
you realize that God
simply gives and imparts
without demanding
anything in return.

178

When you're inspired,

you reconnect to your Source of Being.

You go beyond

the world of limitations

and enter a space

of creative knowing.

179

Any problem
represents your inability
to consciously connect
*to your Source
in the moment.*

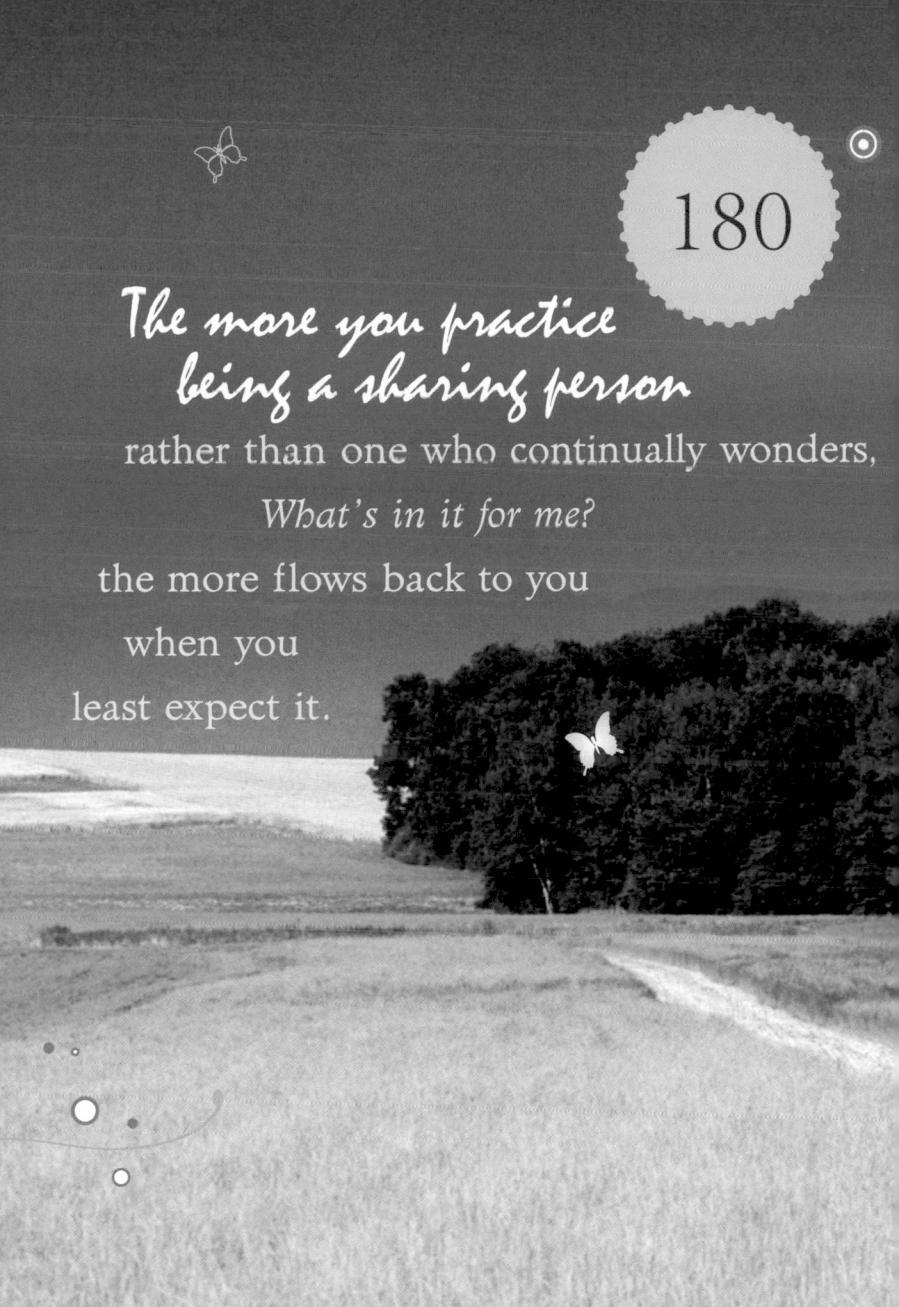

180

**The more you practice
being a sharing person**

rather than one who continually wonders,

What's in it for me?

the more flows back to you

when you

least expect it.

181

When inspiration makes
its presence known,
you must pay attention
if your priority is
to be who or what
you were meant to be.

182

Invite into your heart
only those energies
*that resonate
with the desire*
to obey your ultimate calling
to inspiration.

183

The journey to your
ultimate calling
isn't a scholastic endeavor—
there are no written exams,
no grades to earn,
no report cards,
and no
advanced degrees.

184

As you move into
a state of inspiration
by feeling connected
to a great purpose
or an extraordinary
project,
you surrender.

185

By demonstrating a 100 percent commitment to truth, you send out a signal that you're in accord with your Source, and you'll do more to inspire others to live and breathe from their own truth than a thousand readings of the Ten Commandments or any other written document.

186

Every time someone
attempts to get you to conform, affirm:
I am an individualized

expression of God.
That's all you need
to remember.

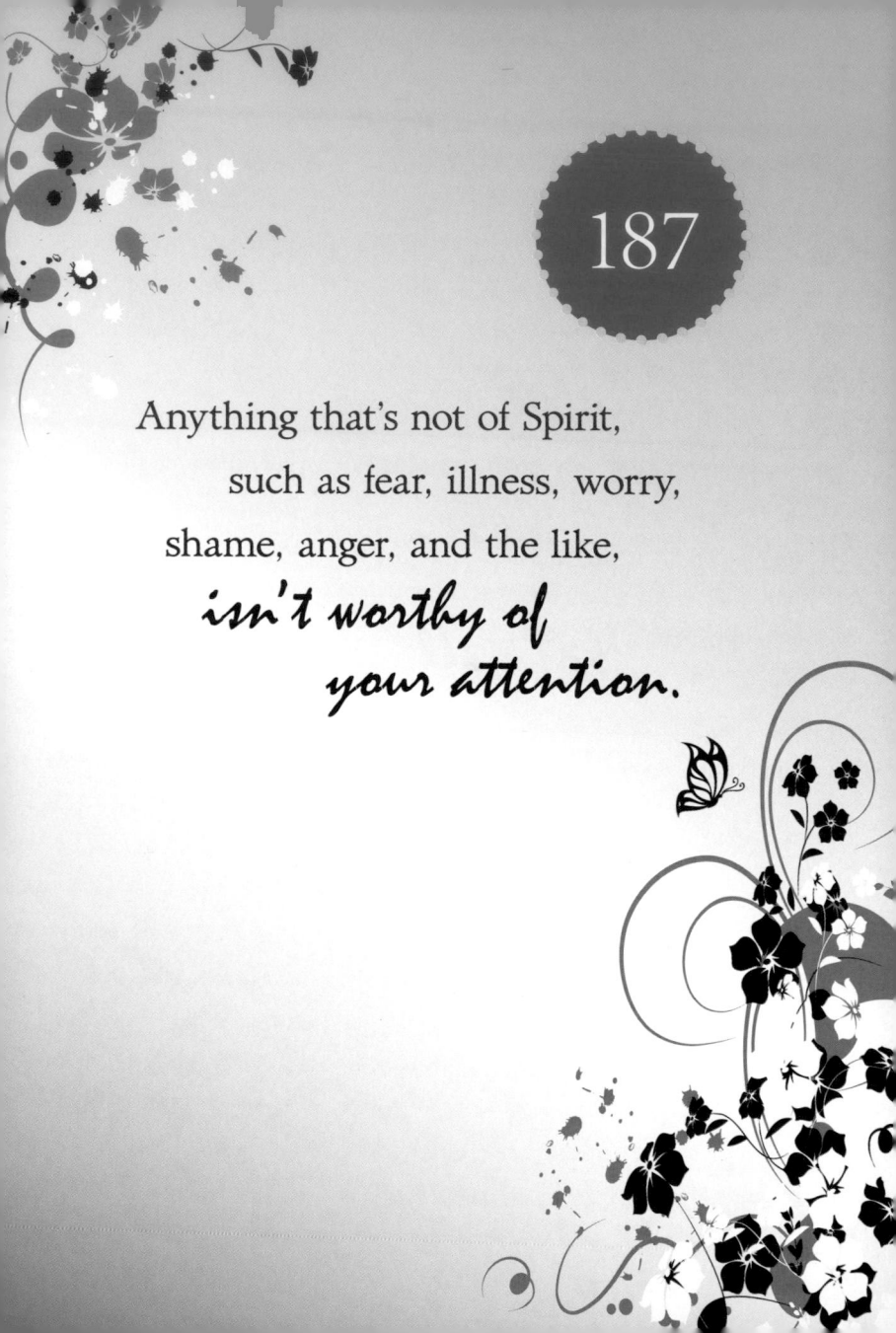

187

Anything that's not of Spirit,
such as fear, illness, worry,
shame, anger, and the like,
*isn't worthy of
your attention.*

188

You needn't focus
on what's already happened
and what you've gone through;
rather, you must
shift your vibration upward
so that it harmonizes with Spirit.
Only then will spiritually based ideas
come knocking on your door.

189

**Faith is an
internal knowing**
that the All-Creating Spirit
provides what you need
precisely on schedule.

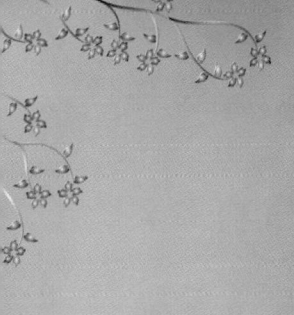

190

Give those who
find fault or who are confrontational
a silent blessing,
and remove yourself
from their energy
as quickly as possible.

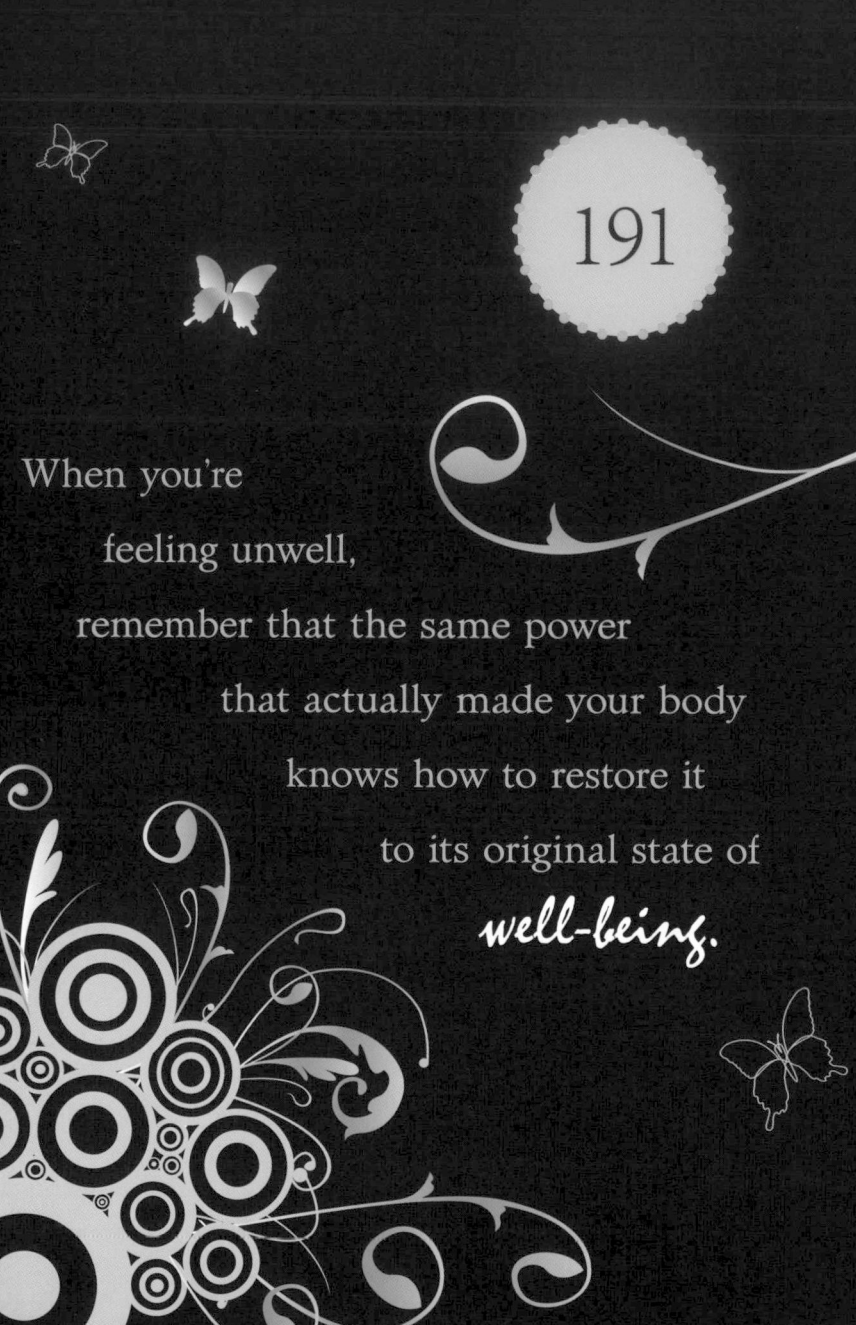

191

When you're
feeling unwell,
remember that the same power
that actually made your body
knows how to restore it
to its original state of
well-being.

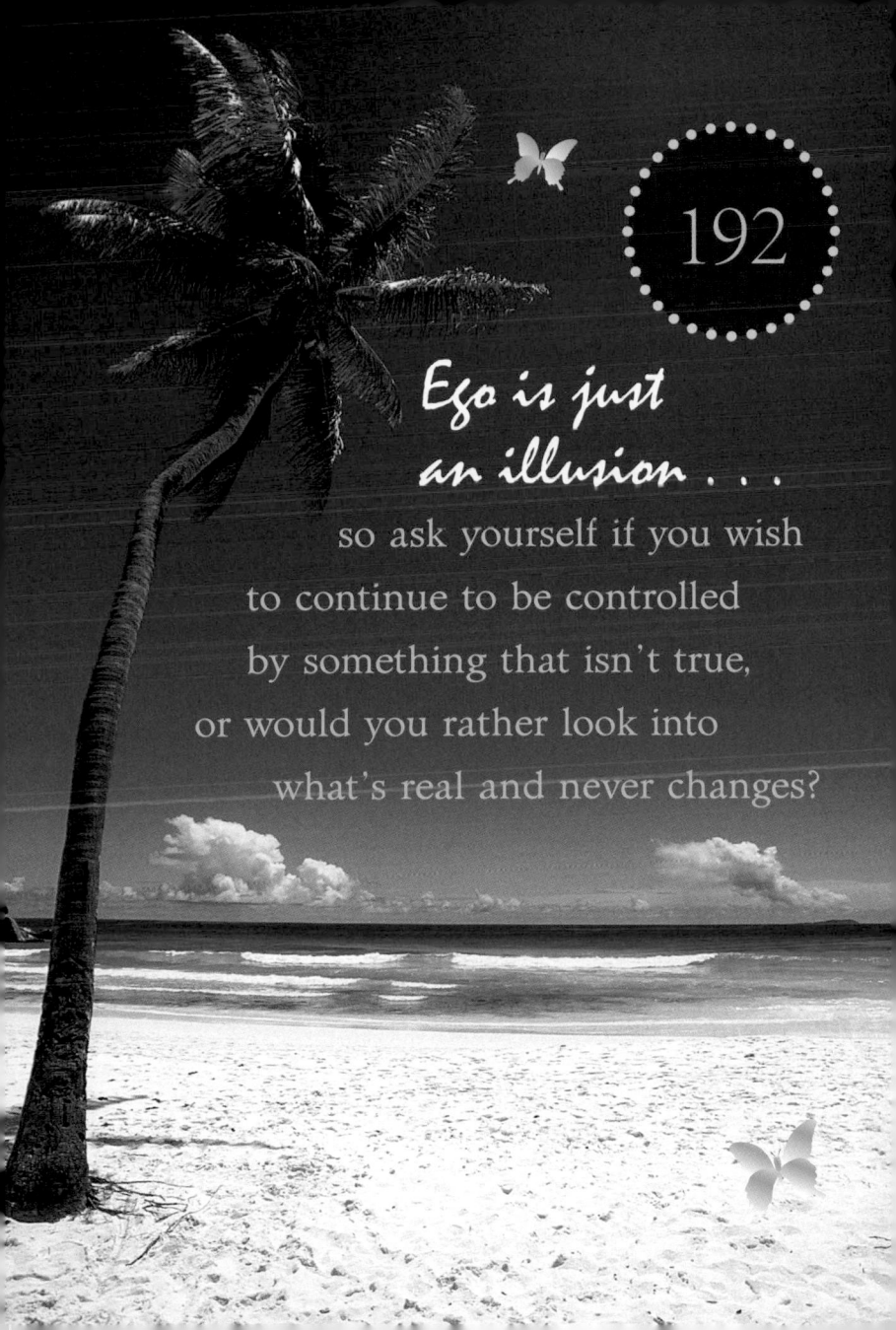

192

Ego is just an illusion . . .

so ask yourself if you wish
to continue to be controlled
by something that isn't true,
or would you rather look into
what's real and never changes?

193

Make a
concerted effort
to allow the
natural-healing
and well-being
capacity
of your body
to play
itself out.

The invisible reality,
where all physical life originates,
is more powerful and significant
than the tiny parenthesis in eternity
that you call "life,"
or what comes
between birth and death.

195

Commit to at least one daily experience

where you share

something of yourself

with no expectation

of being acknowledged

or thanked.

196

Thinking about where
you've been or what you did wrong
in the past are *impediments*
to an inspired life.

197

Deep within you lies an awareness
of what shape your life is to take.
You can hear that voice,

*but first you need to surrender
to that Divine plan*
you signed up for before your conception.

198

There's a force in
the Universe
that's 100 percent trustworthy.
It creates and manifests from love,
cooperation, beauty, and expansiveness,
and it's to this flawless work of Spirit
that you can return
*in order to know
inspiration.*

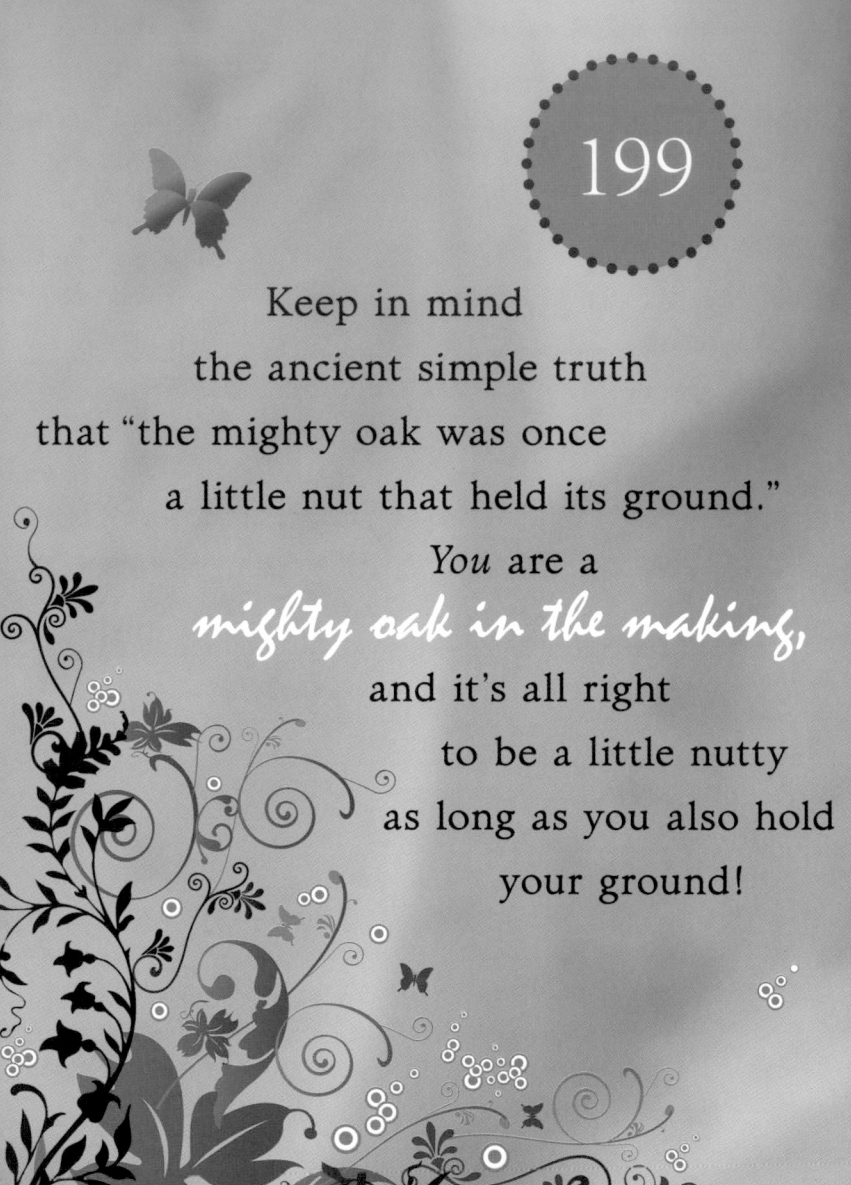

199

Keep in mind
the ancient simple truth
that "the mighty oak was once
a little nut that held its ground."
You are a
mighty oak in the making,
and it's all right
to be a little nutty
as long as you also hold
your ground!

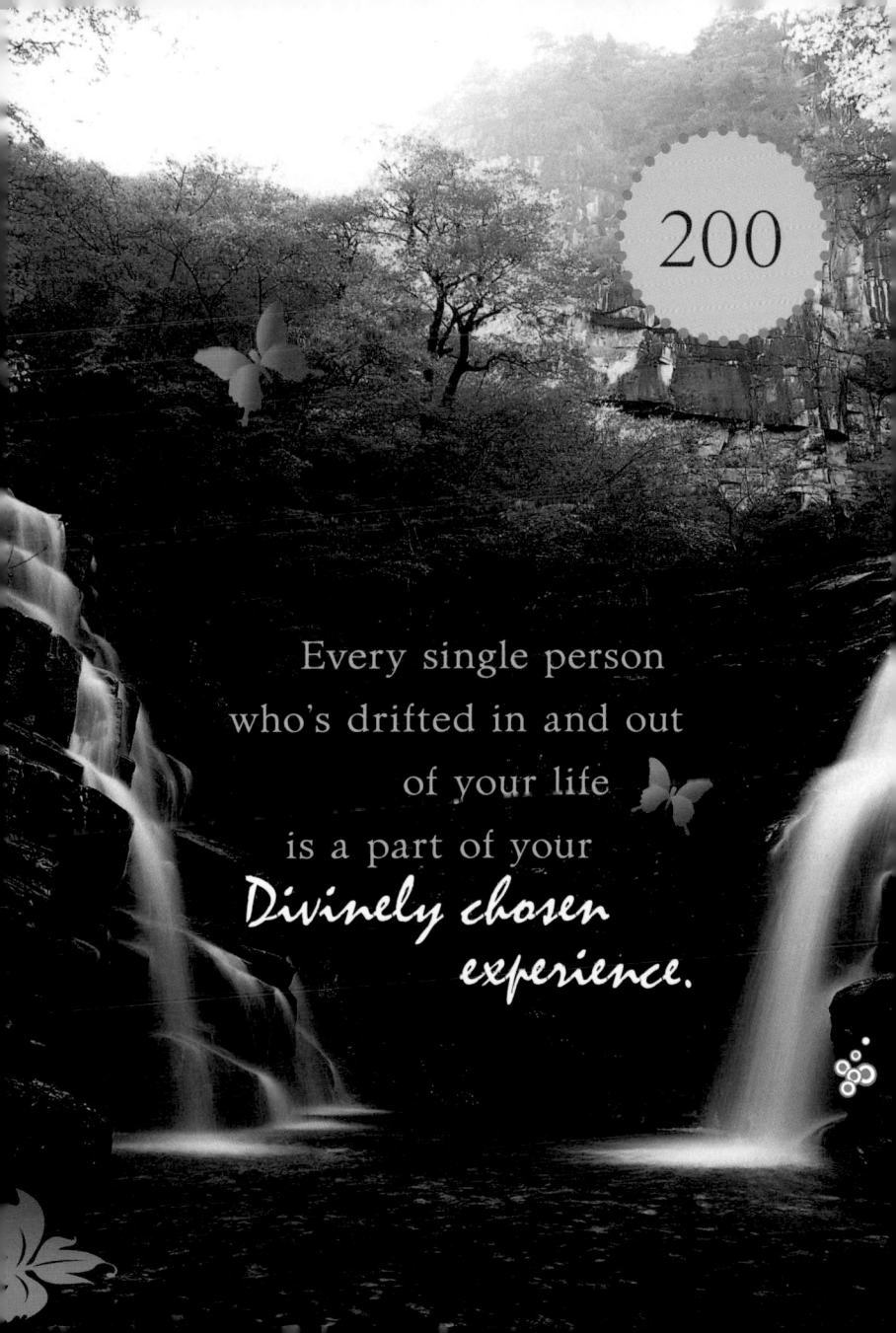

200

Every single person
who's drifted in and out
of your life
is a part of your
*Divinely chosen
experience.*

201

Seek out
"higher-vibrational people,"
and avoid those
who reflect more ego-oriented
behavior patterns.

202

Know that
you are connected
to a continual stream of well-being,
and let this knowing
guide you in all
of your visions for inspiration.

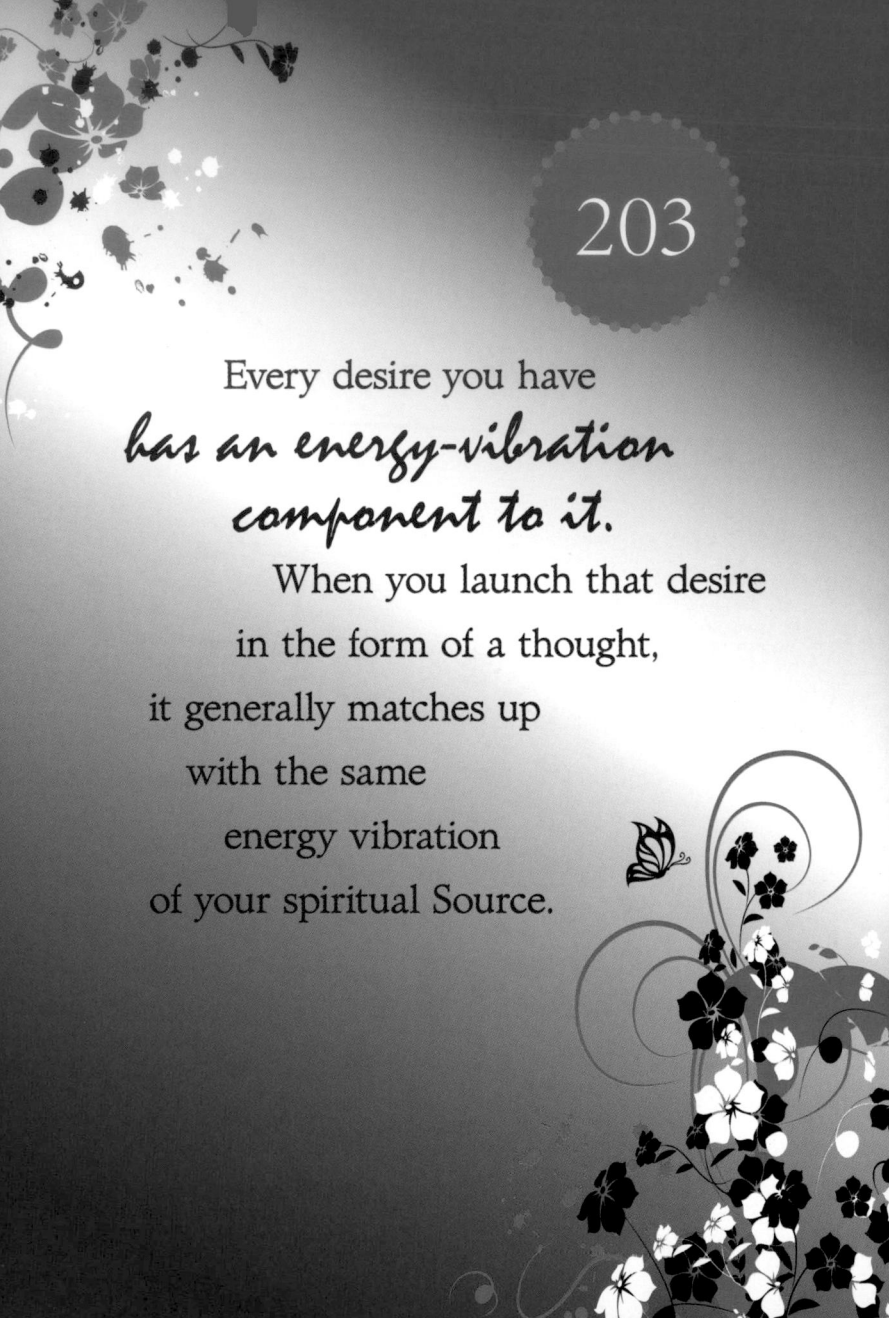

203

Every desire you have
*has an energy-vibration
component to it.*
When you launch that desire
in the form of a thought,
it generally matches up
with the same
energy vibration
of your spiritual Source.

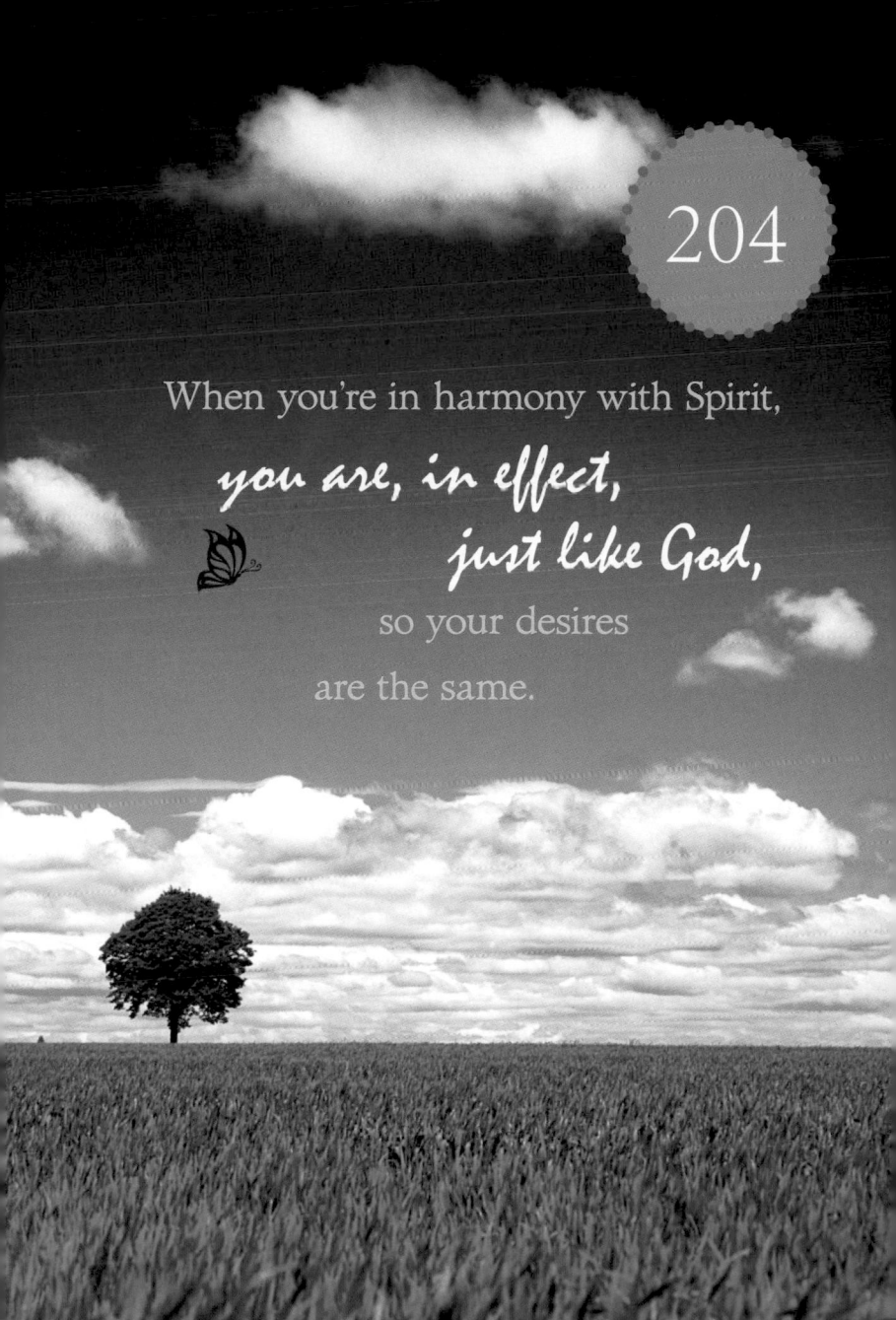

204

When you're in harmony with Spirit,

you are, in effect,

just like God,

so your desires

are the same.

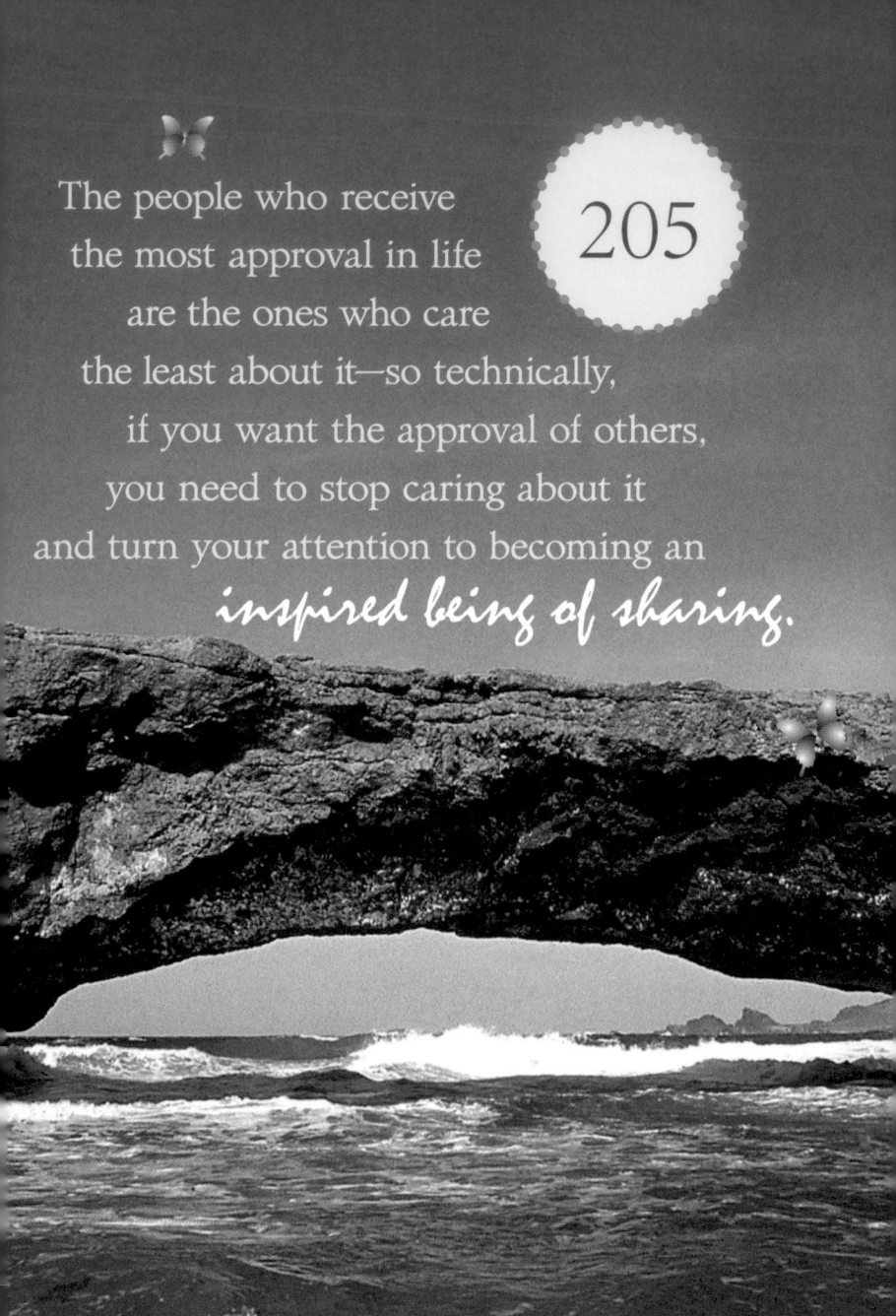

The people who receive
the most approval in life
are the ones who care
the least about it—so technically,
if you want the approval of others,
you need to stop caring about it
and turn your attention to becoming an
inspired being of sharing.

205

206

When you remove the obstacles

erected by you and your toxic world,

you'll allow

true healing power

to flow through you.

207

Your life is

simplified enormously

when you don't have to defend

yourself to anyone,

and when you

receive support

rather than

criticism.

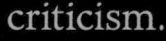

Remember that
you come from
a Source of pure love,
so a simple life means
incorporating that love
as one of the mainstays
of your material

existence.

209

Take stock of those who were
negative forces in your past.
Search for ways in which their actions
might have been

*blessings
in disguise.*

Affirm that

whatever brings passion,

enthusiasm, and inspiration to you

is on its way.

Say it often:

It is on its way, it will arrive on time,

and it will arrive in greater amounts

than I imagined.

211

Give yourself permission

to get away

so that you can camp in the outdoors;

swim in a river, lake, or ocean;

sit by an open fire;

or ski down a mountain slope.

Wherever you live,

you're only a few hours

(or even moments!) away

from being connected

to the entire

Universe.

Practice laughing
at the importance
that you and so many people
place on
everyday circumstances.
View it from an eternal perspective,
and you'll find yourself lightening
that heavy load.

213

When you're *in-Spirit*,
every direction is possible for you
at every moment because your
*consciousness happens
within your mind.*

214

Take more time to hear others.

Notice your inclination
to interrupt and
get the conversation over with,
and then choose
to listen instead.

215

You're in a system
that's directed by
a Supreme Intelligence,
and you're a part
of that system—
that is, *everything is*
on purpose.

Don't make money
the guiding principle for
what you have or do;
rather, simplify your life
and return to Spirit
by finding the inherent value
in everything.

216

217

Know that you,

and all of your fellow

brothers and sisters,

represent God or Spirit

revealing itself

here on our planet.

218

In order to be inspired,
you must maintain
your singular individuality
*while seeing your connection
to your Source*
and to everyone and everything
in the Universe.

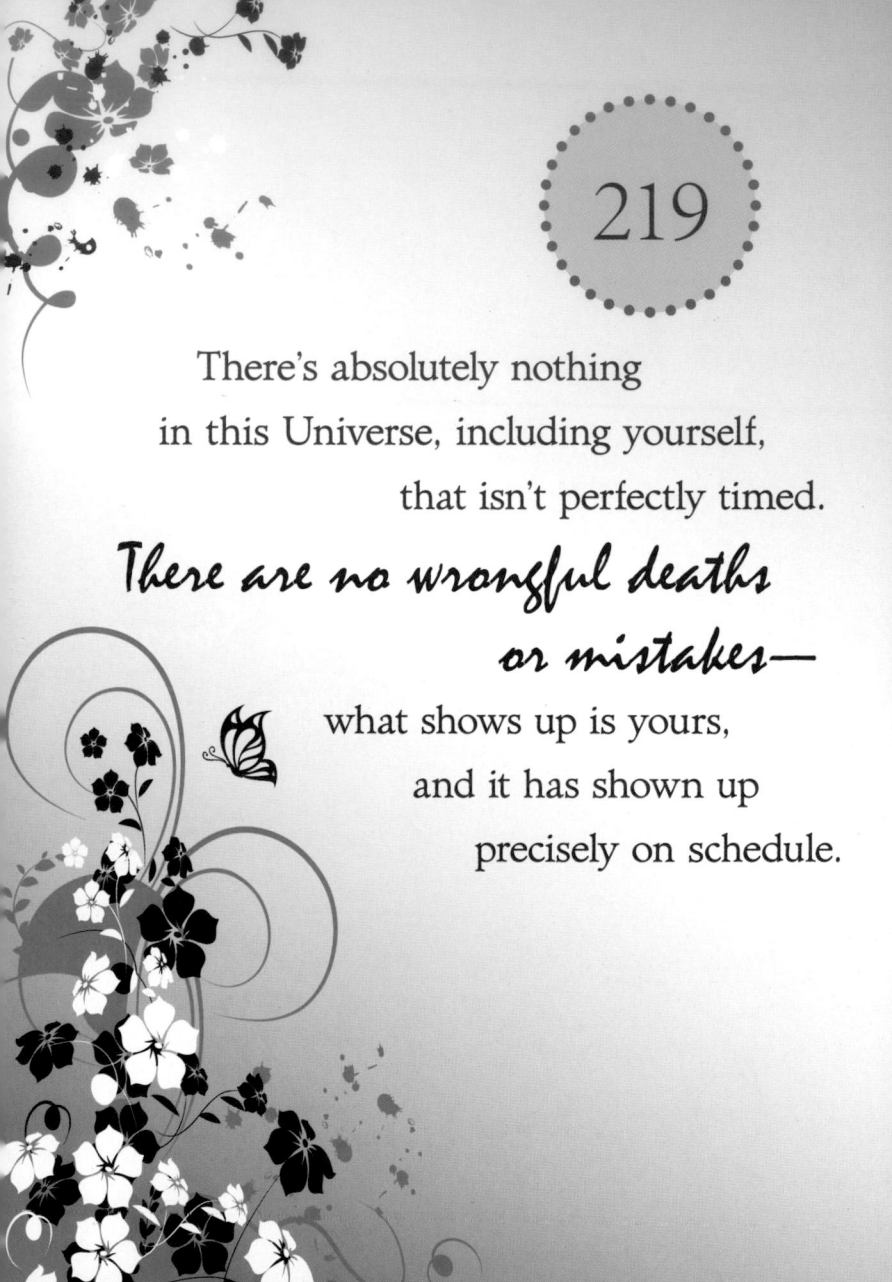

219

There's absolutely nothing
in this Universe, including yourself,
that isn't perfectly timed.
There are no wrongful deaths
or mistakes—
what shows up is yours,
and it has shown up
precisely on schedule.

220

Have quiet interchanges with God,
and know and trust
that spiritual guidance
is available as an
alignment of energy.

You're already connected to everything you need

when you're inspired—what takes place is a realignment within you that allows for every thing, every event, and every person to merge in your "*in-Spirited*" consciousness.

222

Make an attempt
to spend some time each day
in a state of meditation,
wherein you let go of all ideas
about time, space,
and linear directionality.
Just allow yourself to be. . . .

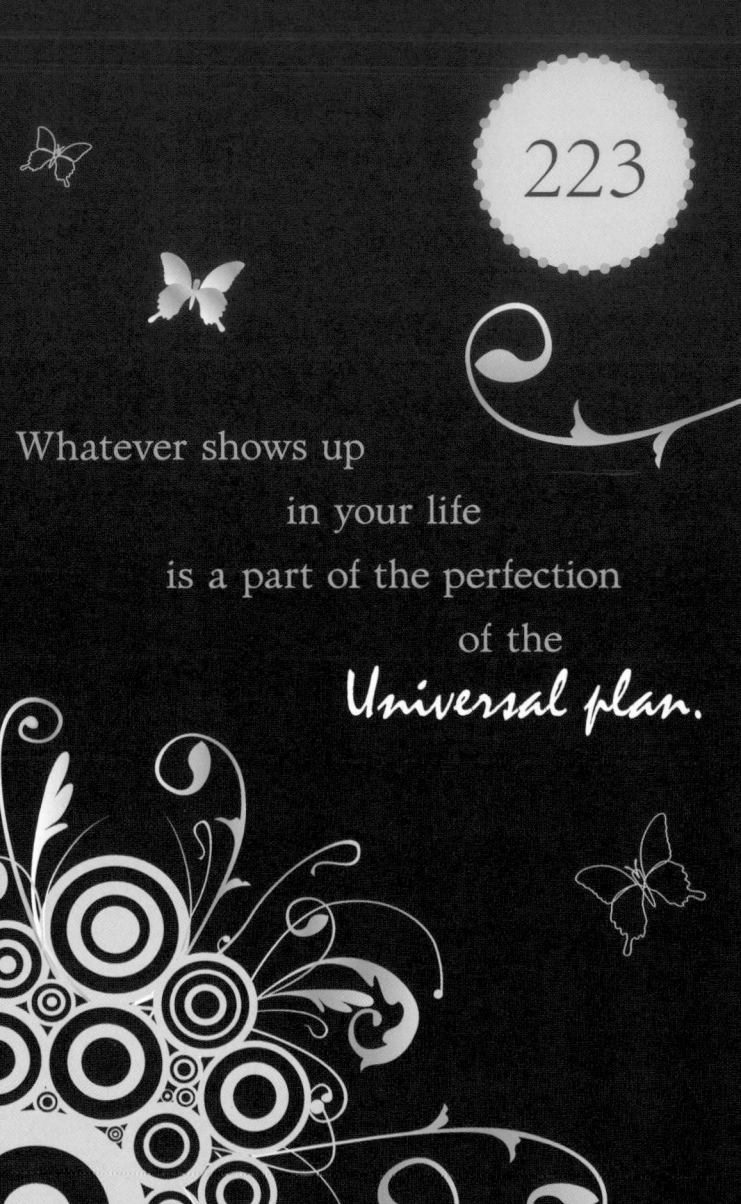

223

Whatever shows up
in your life
is a part of the perfection
of the
Universal plan.

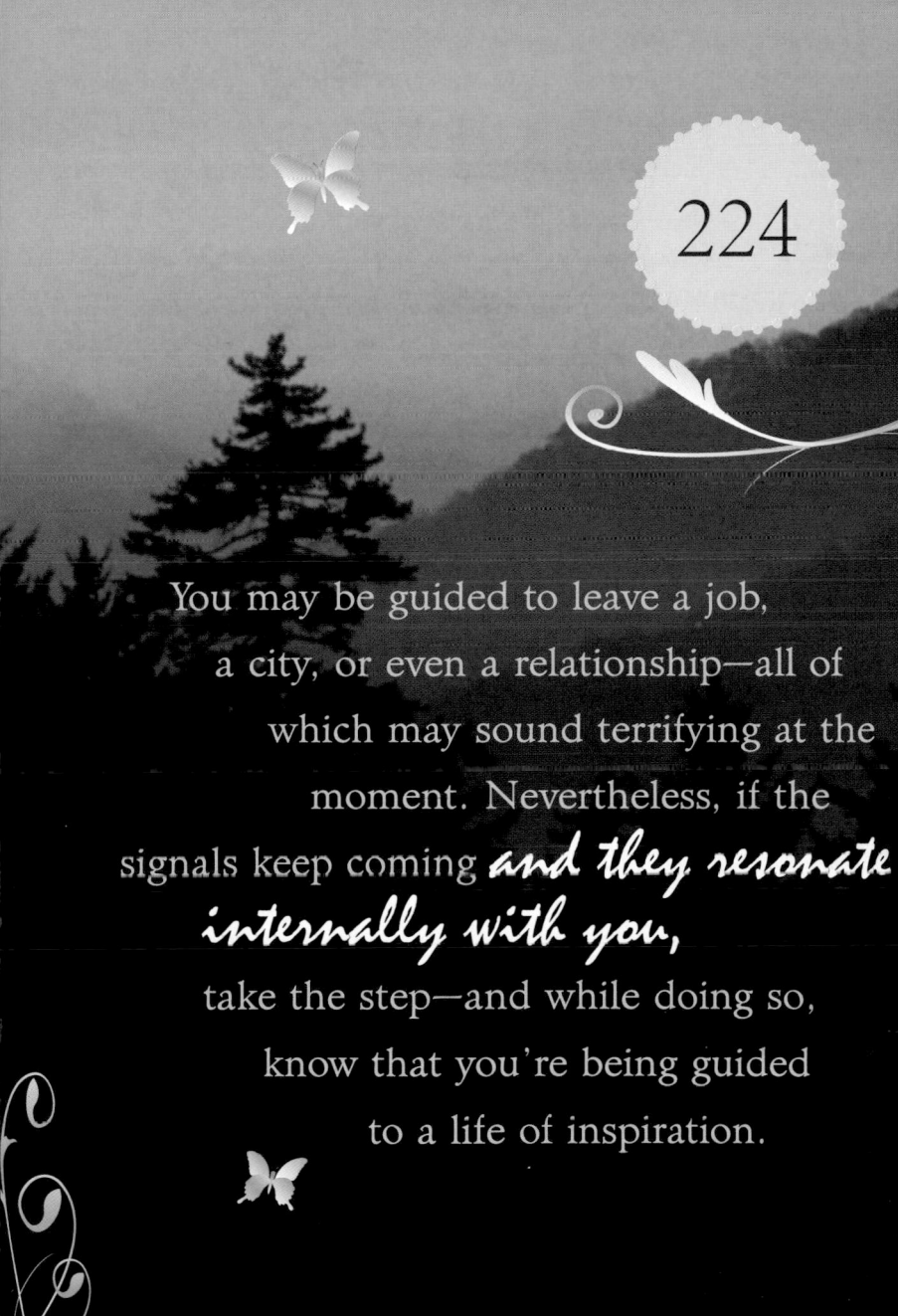

224

You may be guided to leave a job, a city, or even a relationship—all of which may sound terrifying at the moment. Nevertheless, if the signals keep coming *and they resonate internally with you,* take the step—and while doing so, know that you're being guided to a life of inspiration.

225

View uninspired
thoughts
and actions
as impinging
on *your* well-being
and that
of *all* humanity.

When seeking

a teacher,

be on the lookout

for mistaking intellectualization

for inspiration.

A person may have

the highest intellectual credentials available

and still be detached

from his or her spirit.

227

*You can start
returning to being in-Spirit*
by examining what ego
has accomplished in your life,
as well as making
a determined effort to resist
the powerful pressures
of *your culture's* ego
in favor of
an inspired life.

228

Deep within,
you know that the only thing
that's truly important
is being in alignment
with Spirit.

229

When you're in the presence
of an inspiring person, you know
that something is happening energetically.
Even though you can't see,
touch, smell, or hear it,

*you know that
you're experiencing a shift*

that makes you feel incredibly good.

230

Realizing that
*ego is a traitor
to your greatness*
is what ultimately
sets you free of its pull.

231

You need to determine
for yourself how
much you've allowed others
to decide issues
such as what you do,
where and with
whom you live,
and even how
you're treated.

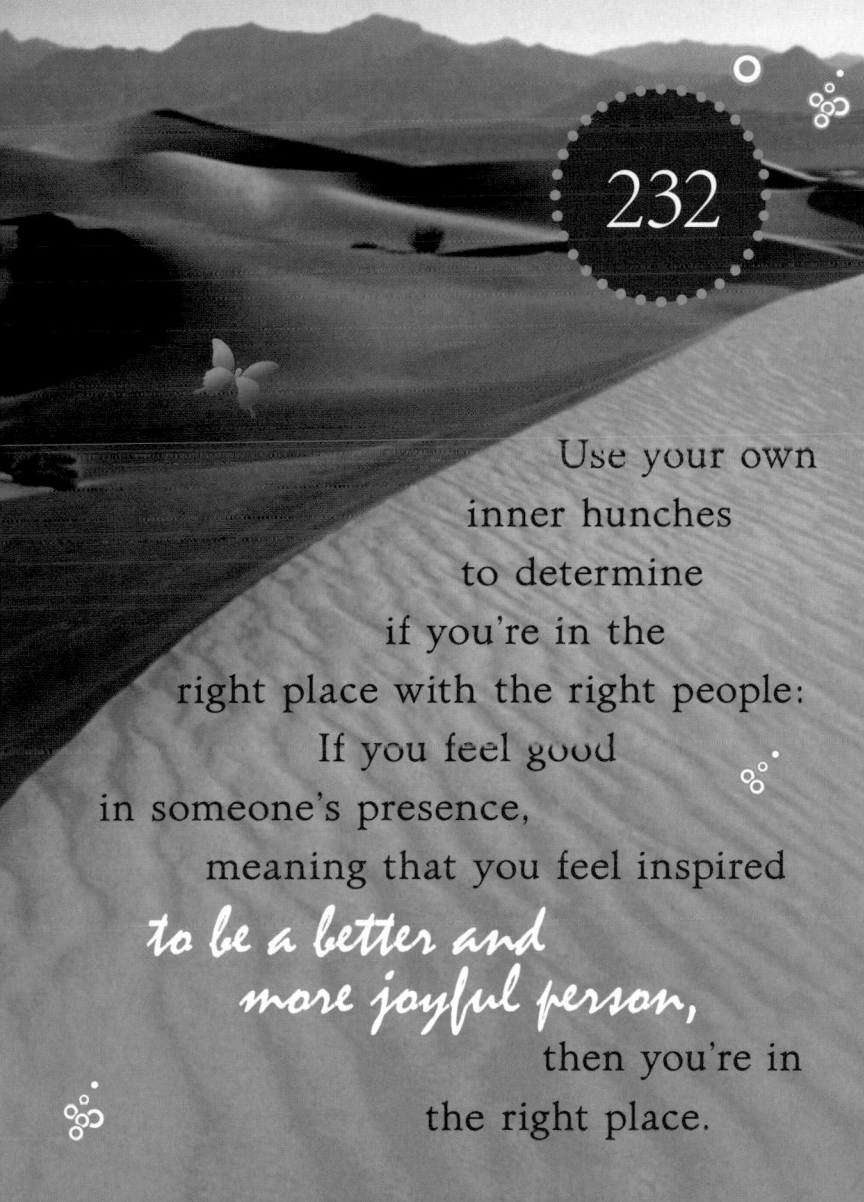

232

Use your own
inner hunches
to determine
if you're in the
right place with the right people:
If you feel good
in someone's presence,
meaning that you feel inspired
*to be a better and
more joyful person,*
then you're in
the right place.

Screen your entertainment options for violence, and make a commitment to choose only those pastimes that are free of any energy that doesn't match your desire to be *in-Spirit*.

233

234

By simply
realigning and harmonizing
with Spirit,
you let inspiration
*blossom in the field
of harmony.*

235

Spiritual teachers have raised
the vibrational frequency
of their daily lives
to the point where they're able
to provide inspiration
to others merely
by their presence,
and this is
the standard to which

*you need
to aspire.*

236

The phrase *I expect miracles* is
more than a New Age slogan,
it's how you feel when you live
each day *in-Spirit*.
You leave the world of
anxiety, fear, doubt,
and impossibility and

enter a new, wonderful world

where all things are possible.

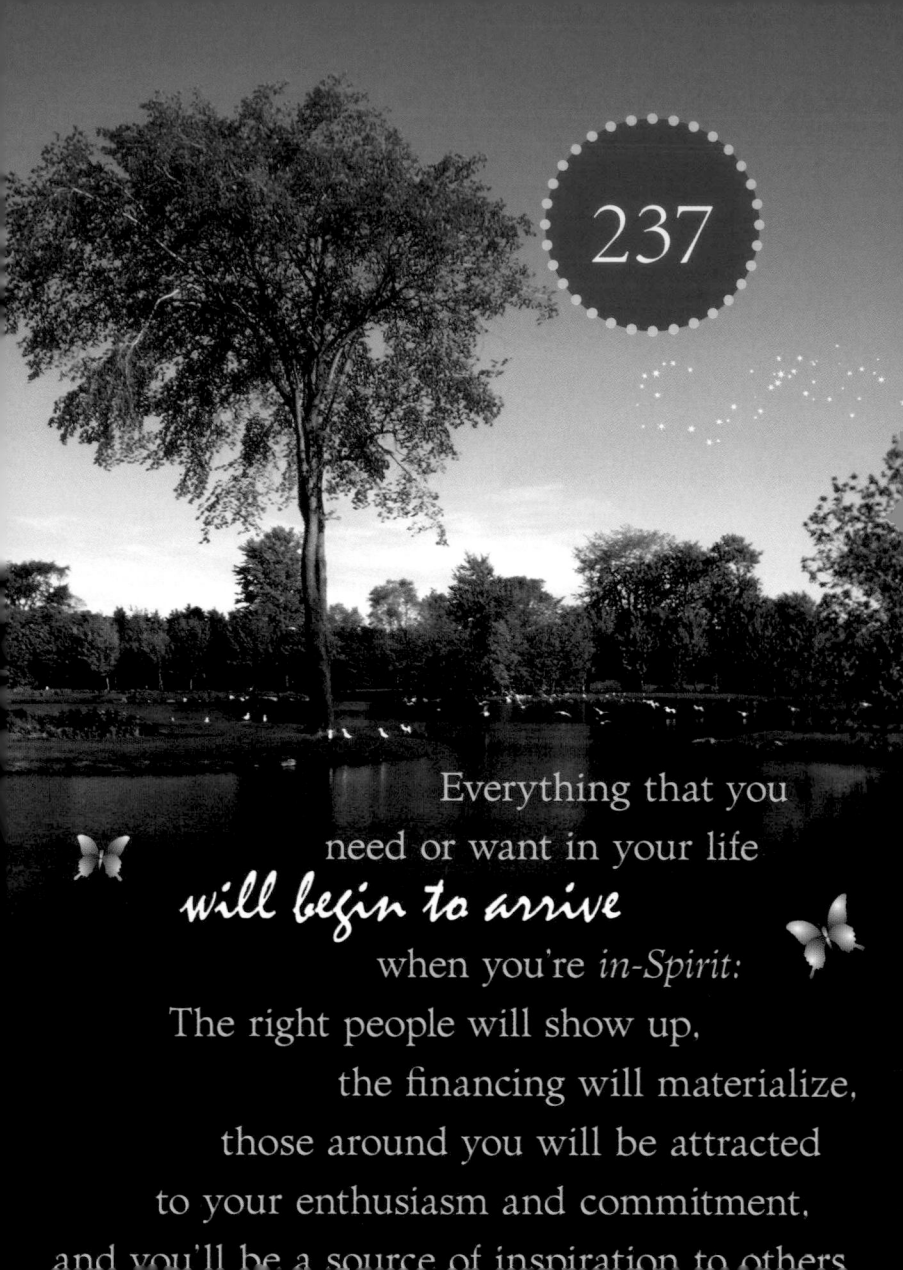

237

Everything that you
need or want in your life
will begin to arrive
when you're *in-Spirit:*
The right people will show up,
the financing will materialize,
those around you will be attracted
to your enthusiasm and commitment,
and you'll be a source of inspiration to others

238

If you practice gratitude
as opposed to maintaining
an attitude of entitlement,
you'll automatically
extend inspiration
wherever you go.

239

Overcome
your inertia.

Since to be inert
is to be without action,
agree to become a being of movement:
Plan to exercise,
make that call
you've been avoiding,
or write that letter.

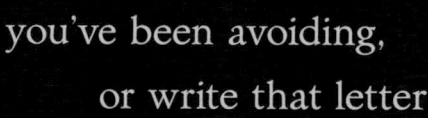

240

In the morning before you're fully awake,

and again as you're going to sleep,

take one or two minutes of

quiet time with God.

Be in a state of appreciation

and say aloud,

"I want to feel good."

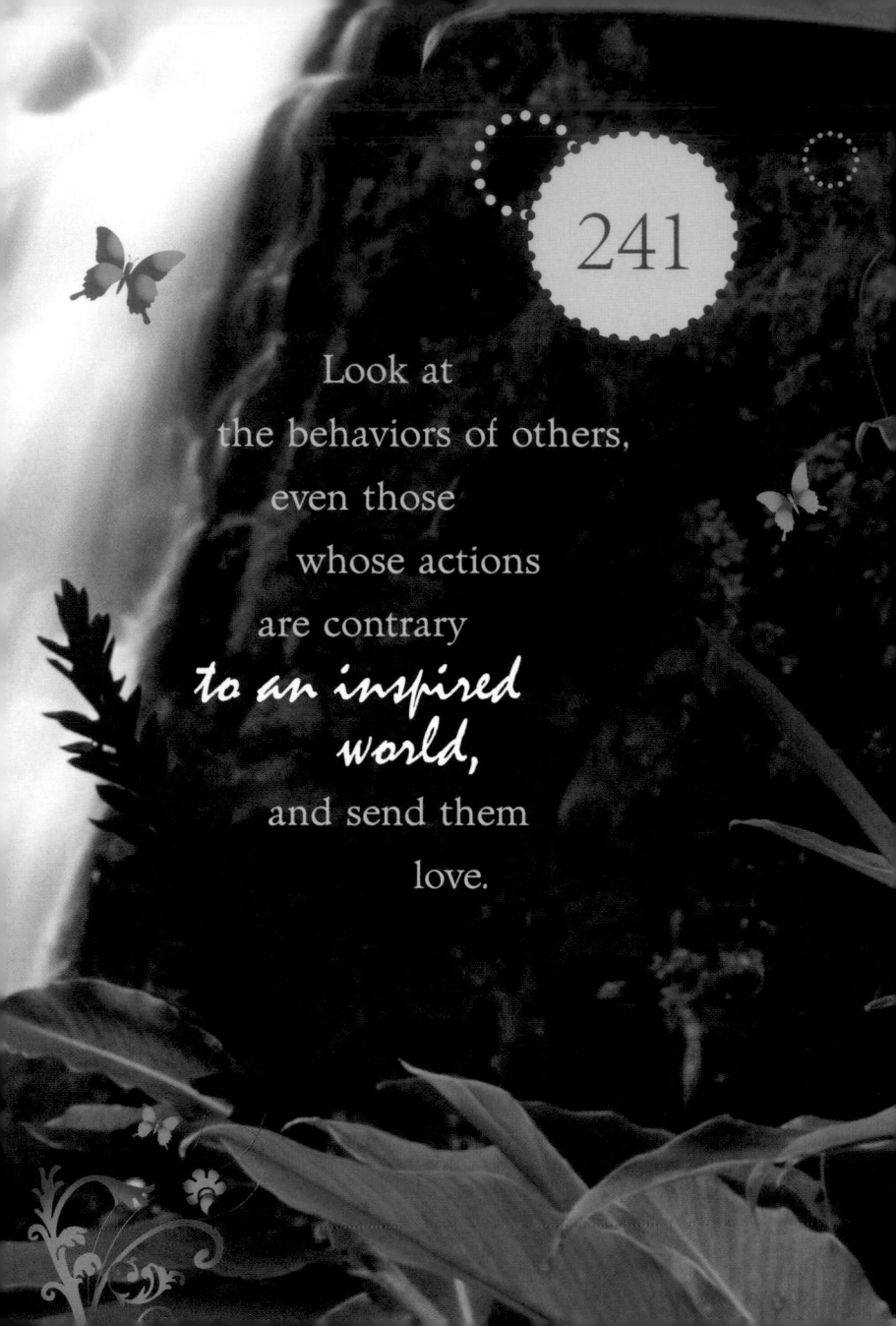

241

Look at
the behaviors of others,
even those
whose actions
are contrary
*to an inspired
world,*
and send them
love.

There's no way
to be *in-Spirit* without
a changed awareness—
so when you accomplish this,
you give yourself the gift of moving
from being flawed, limited, lacking,
and imperfect to being
*completely comfortable
with your magnificence.*

243

Your mind knows
that you're in a Universe
that has a creative,
organizing Intelligence supporting it,
and you know that

*it flows
through you.*

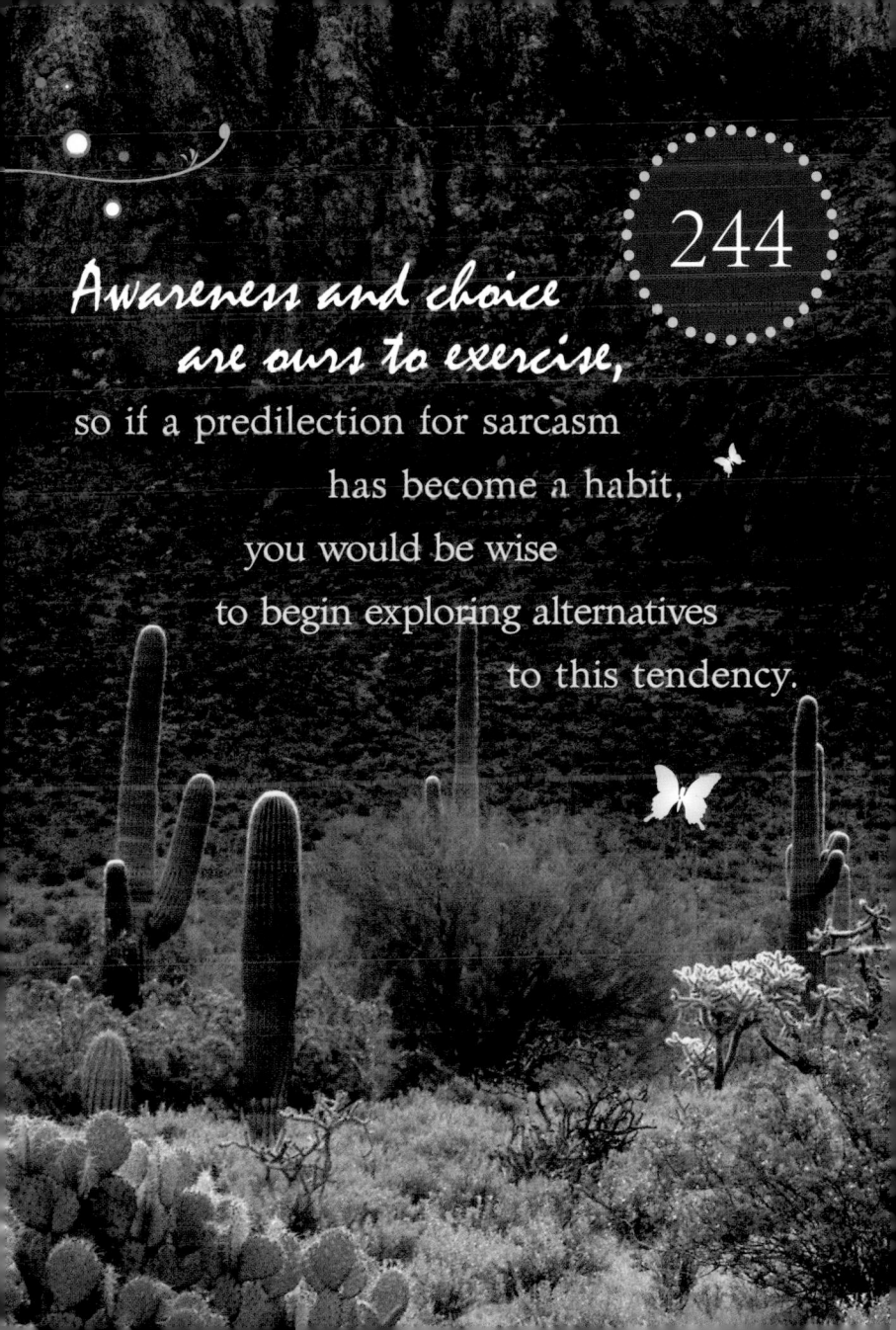

244

Awareness and choice
are ours to exercise,
so if a predilection for sarcasm
has become a habit,
you would be wise
to begin exploring alternatives
to this tendency.

245

The act of being inspired
by some great purpose
allows you to feel
the essence of a spiritual being
having a human experience,
rather than the
other way around.

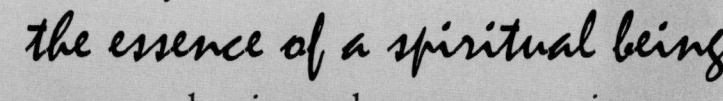

246

Gratitude and humility
send signals to all who
meet and greet you
that you're connected
to something larger
than life itself.

247

Peace doesn't necessarily mean
being in a place
where there's no noise or trouble;
rather, it means that
in the *midst* of turmoil,
you can still feel calm.

248

When you live as much as possible
in God-realization,
nothing can go wrong.
What and whom you need
will surface, and you'll notice
that you can't escape feeling
that something much greater
than your individual life
is at work within and around you.

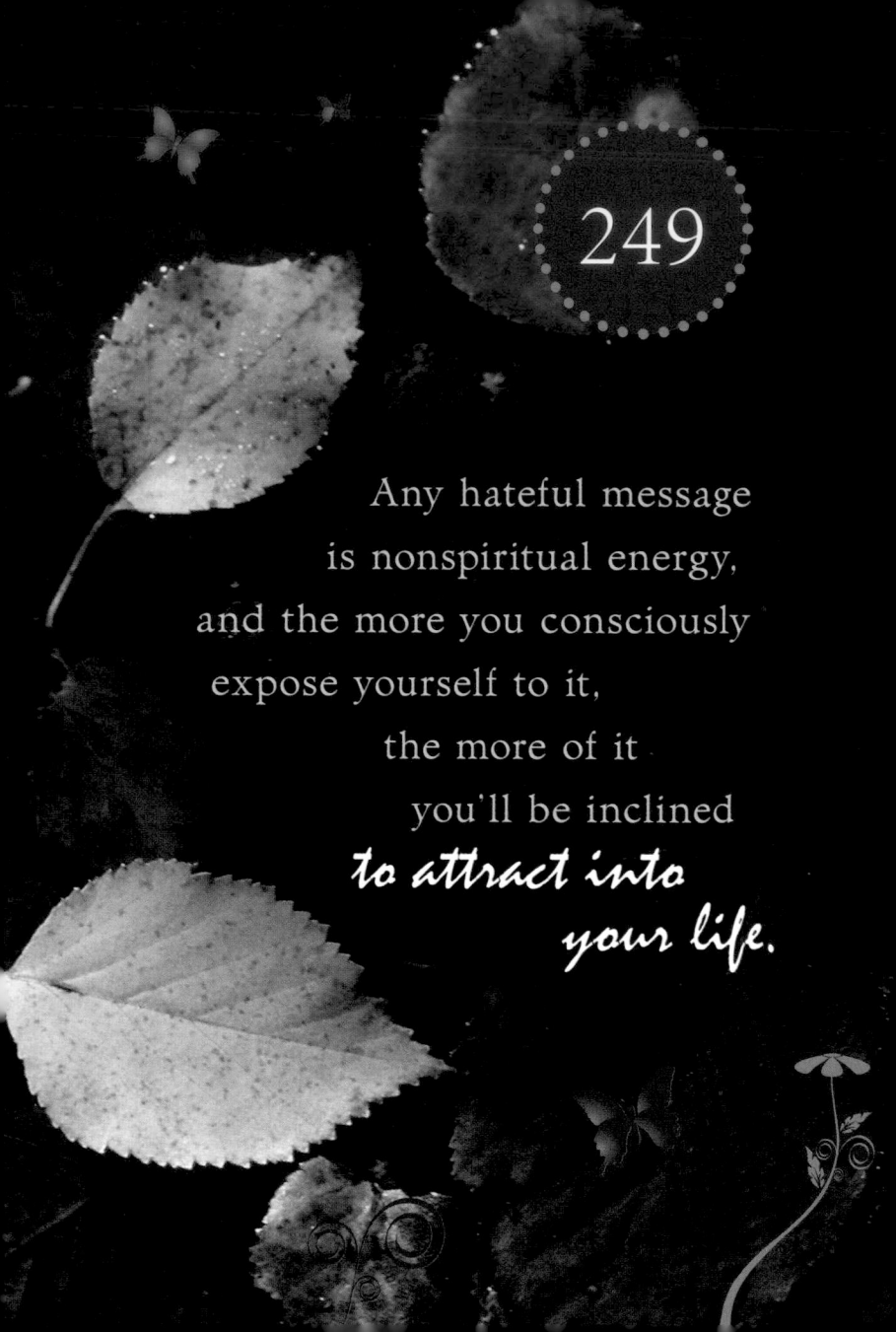

249

Any hateful message
is nonspiritual energy,
and the more you consciously
expose yourself to it,
the more of it
you'll be inclined
*to attract into
your life.*

250

You can shift your vibrations,

in the form of thoughts,

to those that are more harmonious

with your desires,

and you can then begin

to take the small steps necessary

for your inspiration

to be sensed.

251

By keeping your vibration
aligned spiritually,

you see the ecstasy in the present.

Everything else that once
was a source of worry
doesn't come up for you,
since the outcomes are already
handled for you
in your own mind.

252

If you want to move from
disenchantment to inspiration,
or from apathy and indifference
to passion and enthusiasm,
then it's necessary to
*alter your awareness
of yourself.*

253

When you're inspired,
*you're connected
to this Force*
that's greater
in every respect
than your
physical being.

254

There are many people in the world
who seem to be motivated by evil,
but you must be careful
*not to assign power
to a force that doesn't exist.*
There are really only people
moving away from Source
with behavior
that contradicts
the creative energy
that's within them.

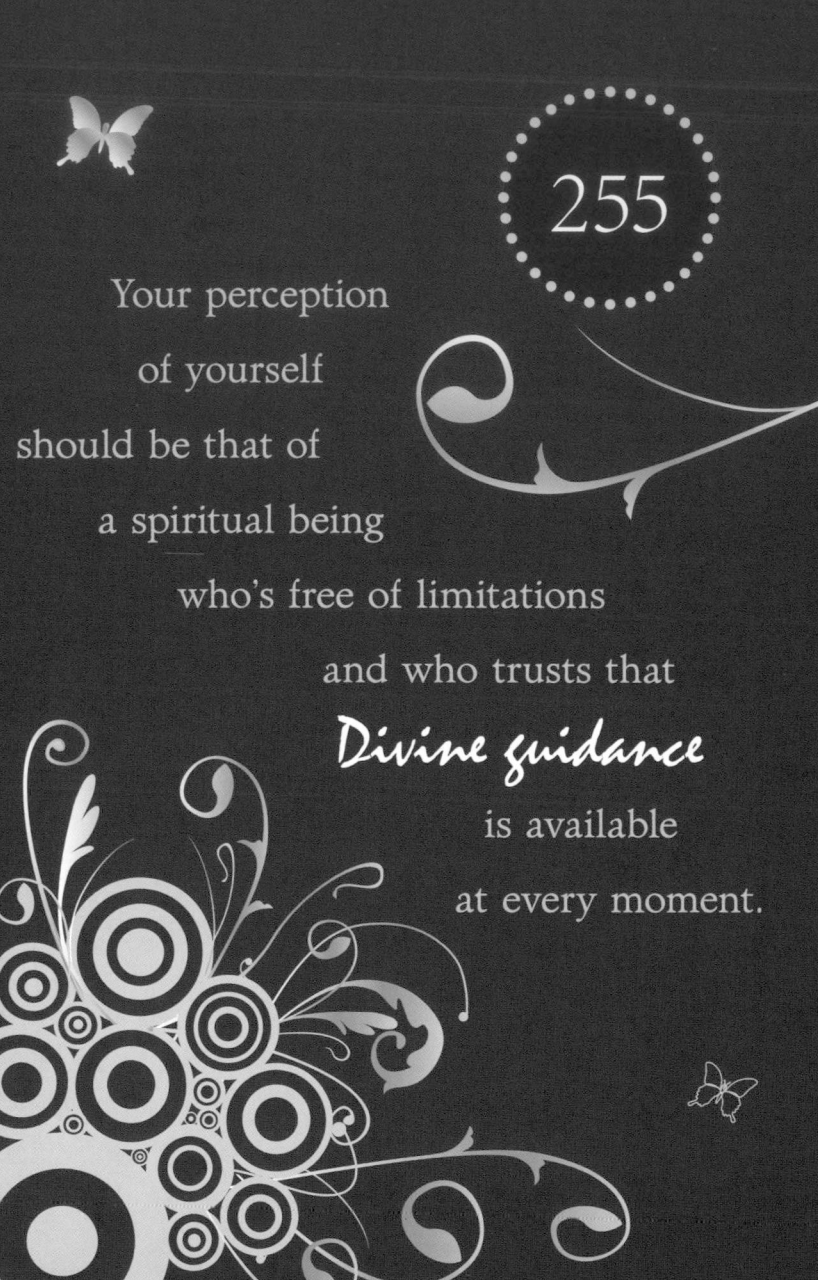

255

Your perception
of yourself
should be that of
a spiritual being
who's free of limitations
and who trusts that
Divine guidance
is available
at every moment.

256

Keep in mind that Spirit *is fixed, permanent, and infinite,* while ego comes and goes with the wind.

257

Remember the words
of Michelangelo:
"The *greater danger*
for most of you
lies not in setting
your aim too high
and falling short;
but in setting your aim
too low,
and achieving
your mark."

258

Develop a private trust

in your ability to activate and

attract dormant forces.

Visualize yourself as a being

who can command these

seemingly inert forces

to work with you.

259

By living
an inspired life,
you're focused on
giving your life away
and simultaneously observing
how it's returned,
thus fortifying
the idea of
"What goes around
comes around."

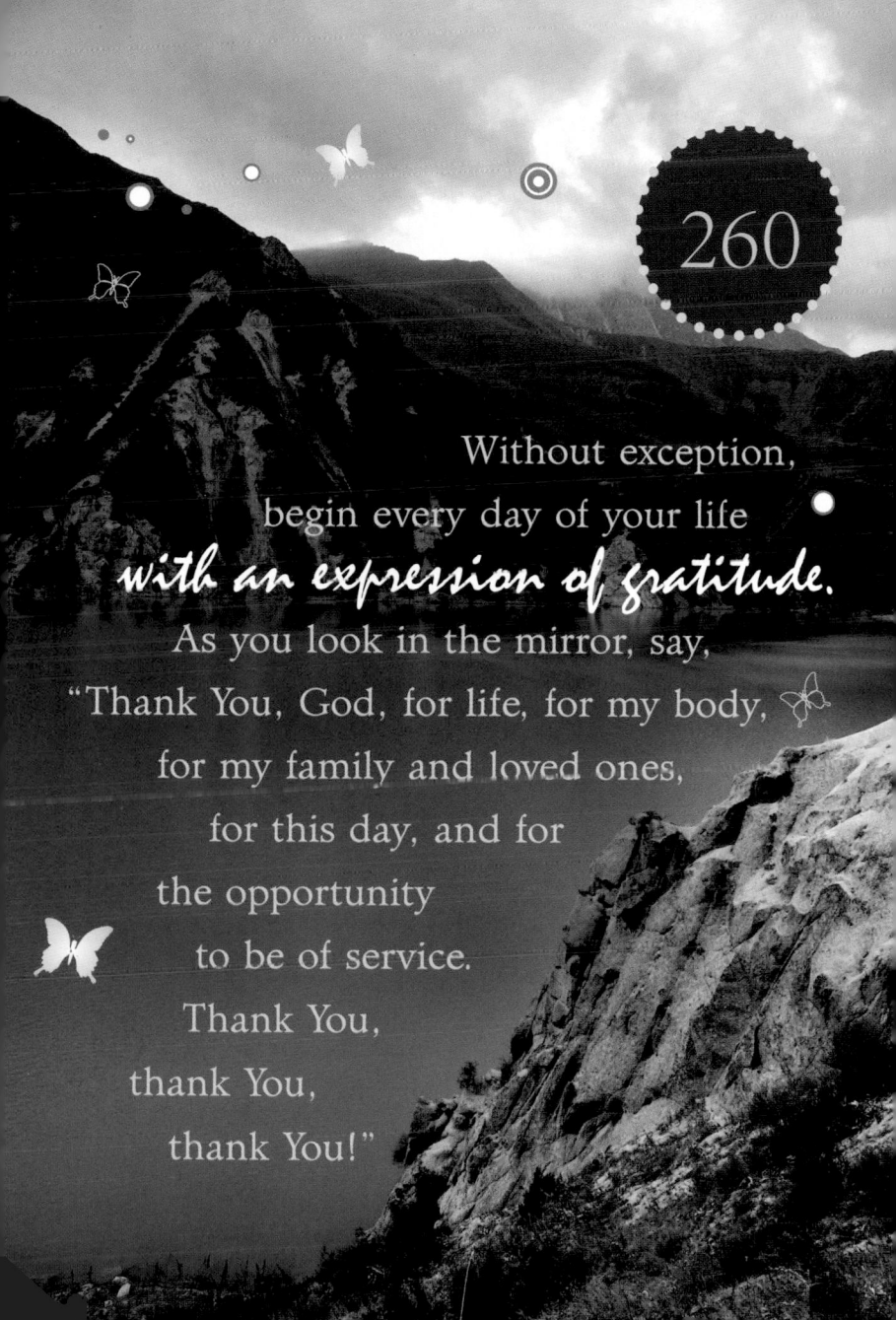

260

Without exception,
begin every day of your life
with an expression of gratitude.
As you look in the mirror, say,
"Thank You, God, for life, for my body,
for my family and loved ones,
for this day, and for
the opportunity
to be of service.
Thank You,
thank You,
thank You!"

261

You came from a quiet, peaceful place
that's the very essence of creation,
so when your mind is filled
with noisy dialogue,
you shut out the possibility of
remembering your Spirit.

262

Live your life
knowing that
your true being is deathless.
This is a great comfort,
as you can
leave sorrow behind
and be inspired.

263

You can link up to all-knowingness
by thinking like God—
that is, by being an energetic match
in your thoughts and actions,
by being grateful,
and by thinking
of others
and offering them
what you desire.

264

Just the mere act
of questioning
your ability
to live an inspired life
represents resistance
that you need
to examine because it implies
that you're deficient
in your spiritual quest.

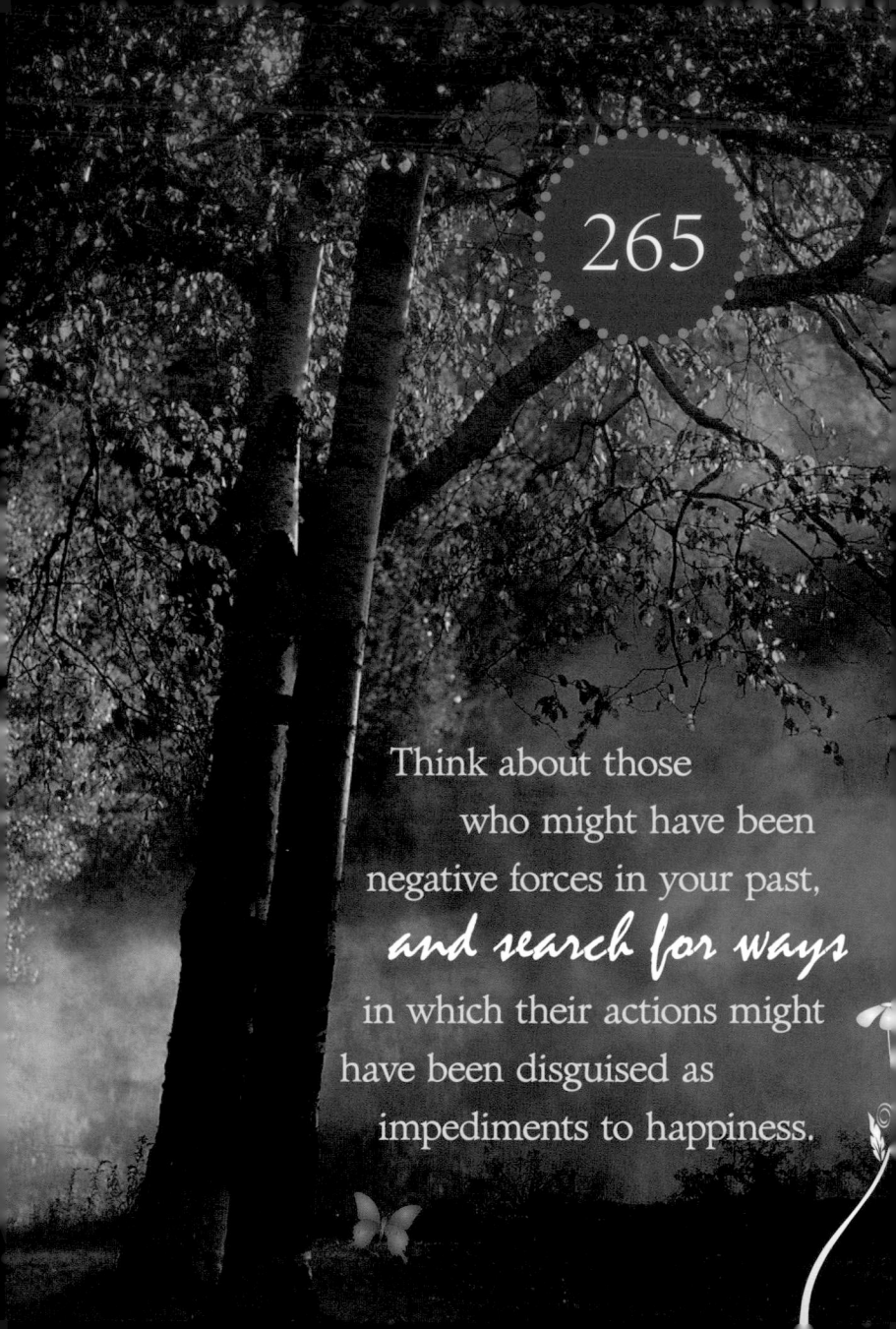

265

Think about those
who might have been
negative forces in your past,
and search for ways
in which their actions might
have been disguised as
impediments to happiness.

266

At your core,

the place where you originate from

and return to,

there's no one

and no thing to judge.

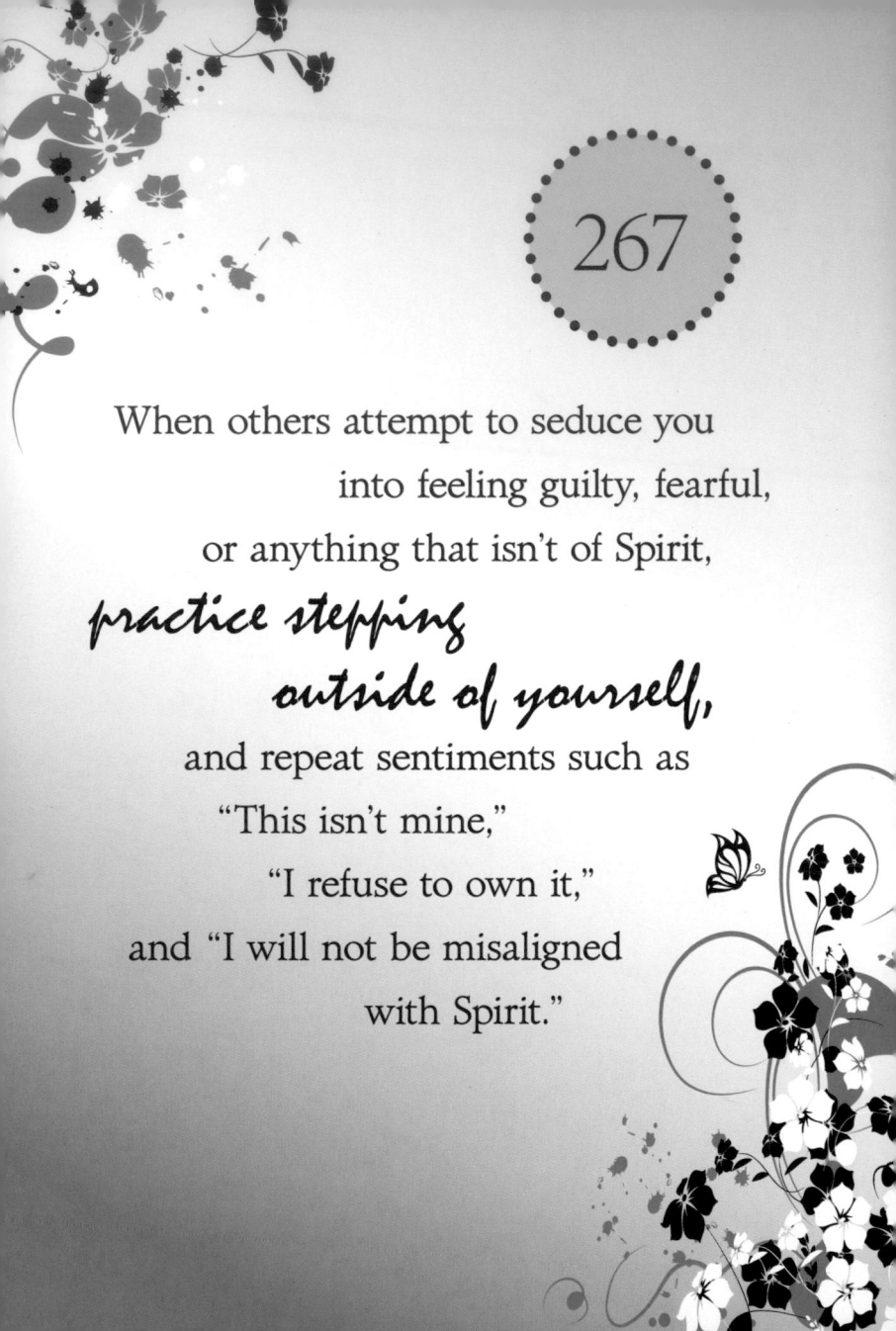

267

When others attempt to seduce you
into feeling guilty, fearful,
or anything that isn't of Spirit,
practice stepping
outside of yourself,
and repeat sentiments such as
"This isn't mine,"
"I refuse to own it,"
and "I will not be misaligned
with Spirit."

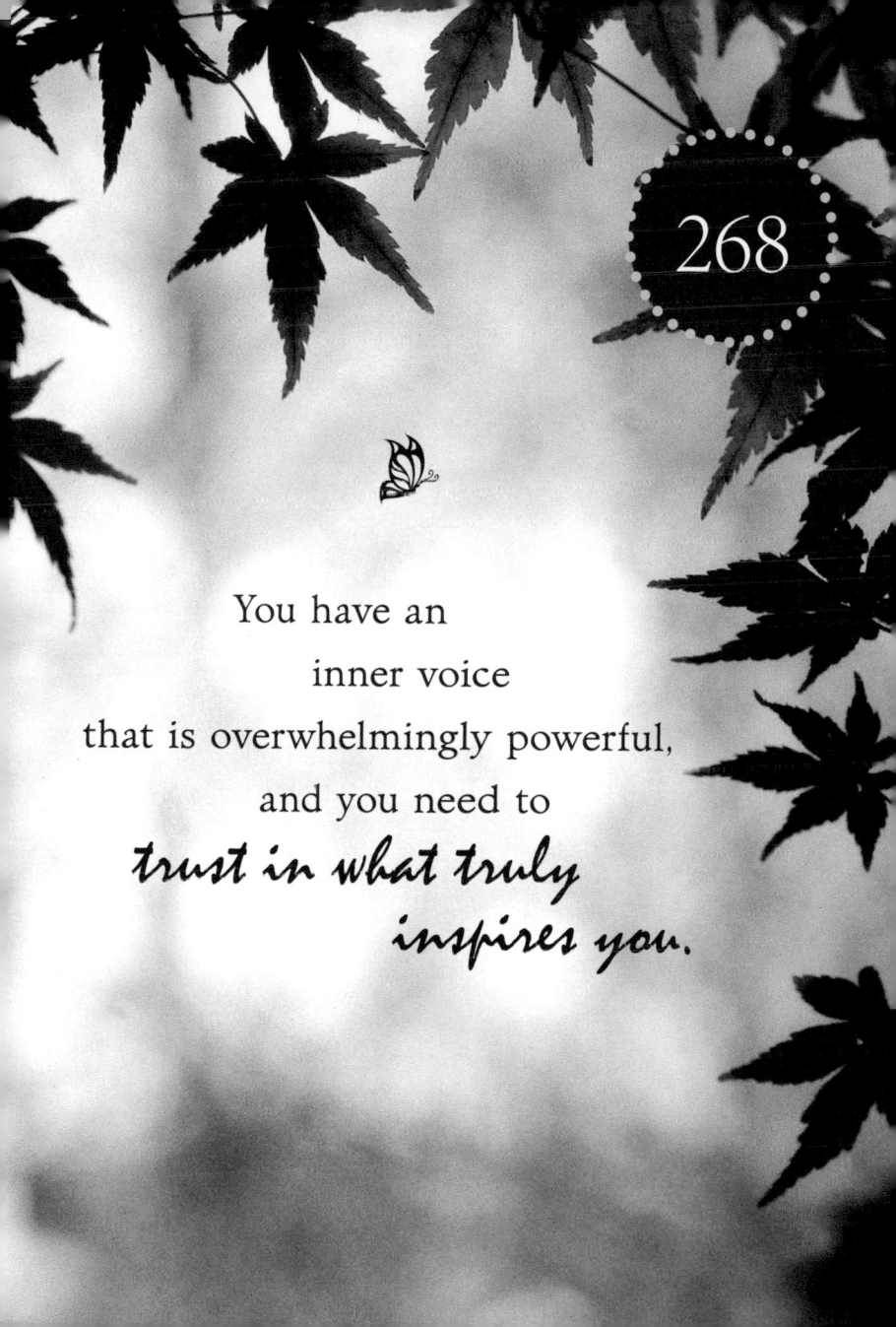

268

You have an
inner voice
that is overwhelmingly powerful,
and you need to
*trust in what truly
inspires you.*

269

When you steadfastly refuse
to think, act,
and conform
to the mandates of others,
the pressure to do so
loses its
momentum.

270

When you go to your Source,
you activate the energy
that reconnects you
to your purpose—
inspiration then shows up
right before your eyes—
even when you may have
stopped thinking about it.

271

All guilt and regret

simply serve as ways

to avoid being here

in the only moment you have,

which is *now.*

272

This is an
intelligent system
that you're
a part of—
*you're a
Divine being*
who is a piece
of the entire pie
of creation.

273

Your purpose in life
isn't to arrive
at a destination where
you find inspiration,
just as the purpose
of dancing isn't to end up at
a particular spot on the floor.
The purpose of dancing
—and of life—
is to enjoy
every moment
and every step,
regardless of where you are
when the music ends.

274

True nobility

is not about being better

than someone else,

it's about being better

than you

used to be.

275

There are no conflicts—

all is as it should be.

The things you wish to improve

aren't going to be accomplished

by fighting,

but by placing your attention

on staying

connected to Spirit.

276

The laws of
the material world
truly do not apply
in the presence
of God-realization,
and you have the choice to
*to live at
this level of inspiration.*

277

By deciding to live an inspired life,

you're choosing to be in balance

with a Creative Force

that responds to your

in-Spirit thoughts.

278

Each time that you're tempted
to try to change people
or situations in your world,
try to catch yourself,
and return to a mind-set
that calls to you to
be more like God,
right here
and right now.

279

Always remember that
when the student is ready,
the teacher will appear.
*Stay in an attitude
of readiness at all times,*
and the teachers and
the teachings will
manifest for you.

280

When an organization
includes some,
yet excludes others,
they're announcing that
they're not actually preaching
or teaching truth.
Since God excludes no one,
any religious organization
that does
isn't affiliated with Him.

281

When you
begin
to question
God's omniscience,
*banish that doubt
from your mind.*

You've got to figure out
how to return to
where you came from
in order to commune
with your Spiritual Creator.
Therefore, being inspired itself
is going to require you
to go back and
do some major
remembering.

The way to *approach God for guidance* and help with

anything

in your life is to do so from

the vantage point of forgiveness—

for others and for yourself.

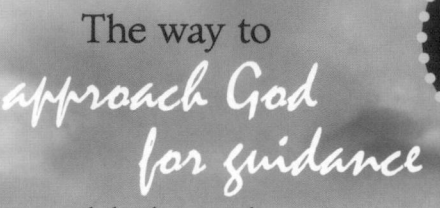

283

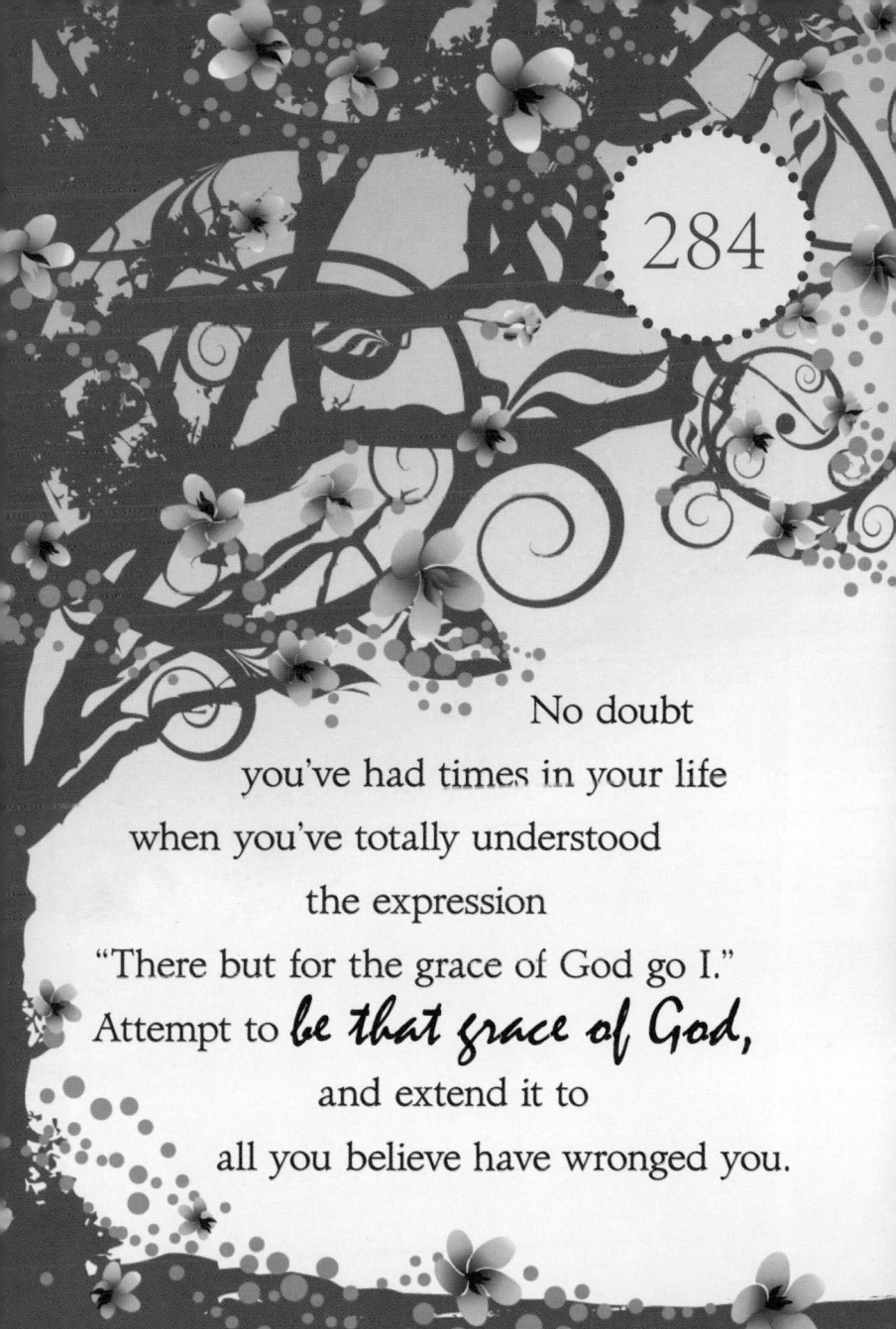

284

No doubt
you've had times in your life
when you've totally understood
the expression
"There but for the grace of God go I."
Attempt to *be that grace of God,*
and extend it to
all you believe have wronged you.

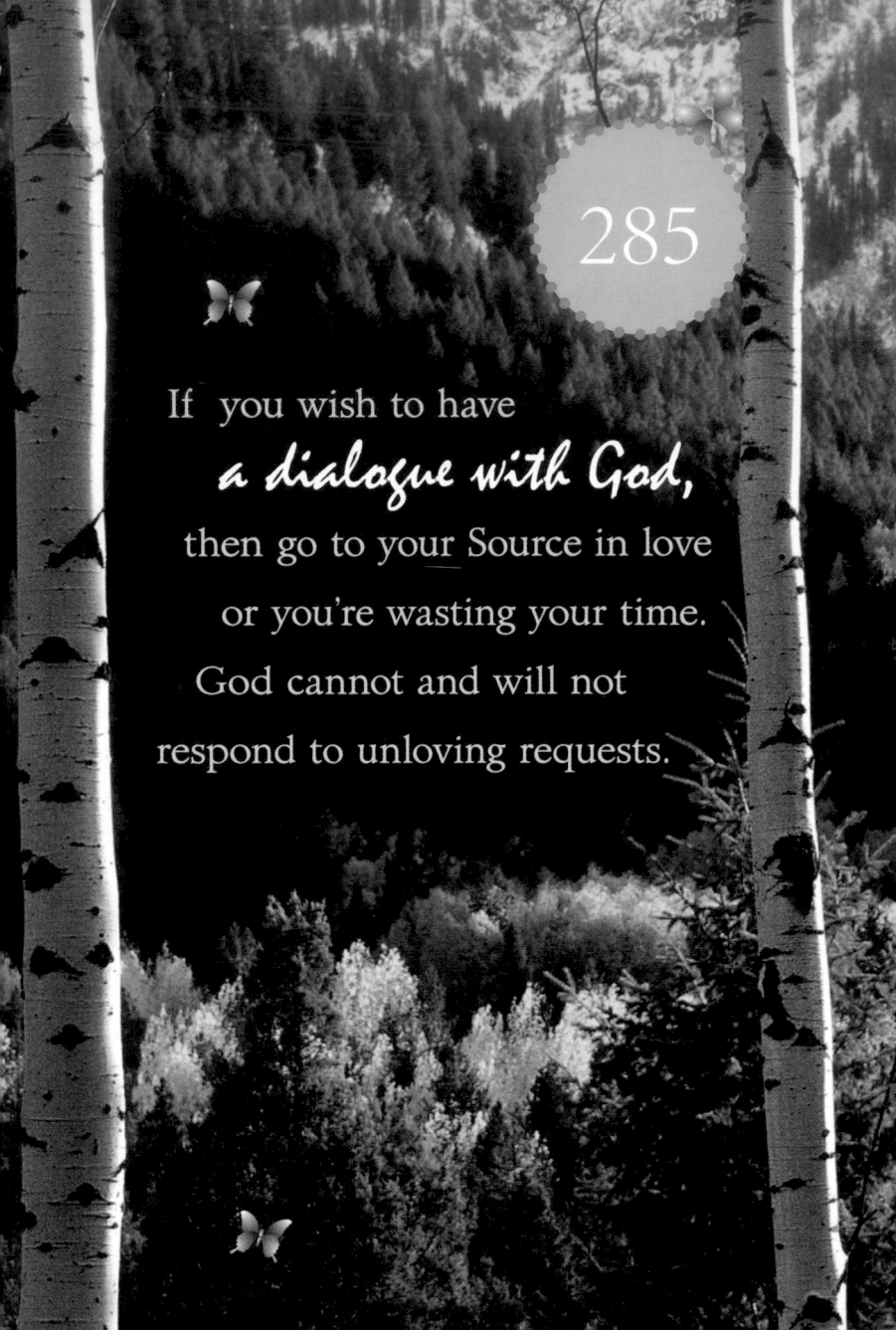

285

If you wish to have

a dialogue with God,

then go to your Source in love

or you're wasting your time.

God cannot and will not

respond to unloving requests.

Your relationship with God, **286** your All-Knowing, Never-Forgetting Senior Partner, is just like your childhood relationship with your parents. Just as you did with your mother and father, *you're now choosing to trust* in the wisdom of your Creator.

287

Never give up on yourself
or feel shame as a result
of not fulfilling
your objective
to serve as a being of inspiration.
Every fall that you take
is a gift,
and every relapse
is a glorious
opportunity.

288

If what you desire
is to be inspired and feel joy,
but the opposite
keeps showing up,
rather than cursing fate,
you can view yourself
as simply being
out of creative
vibrational alignment.

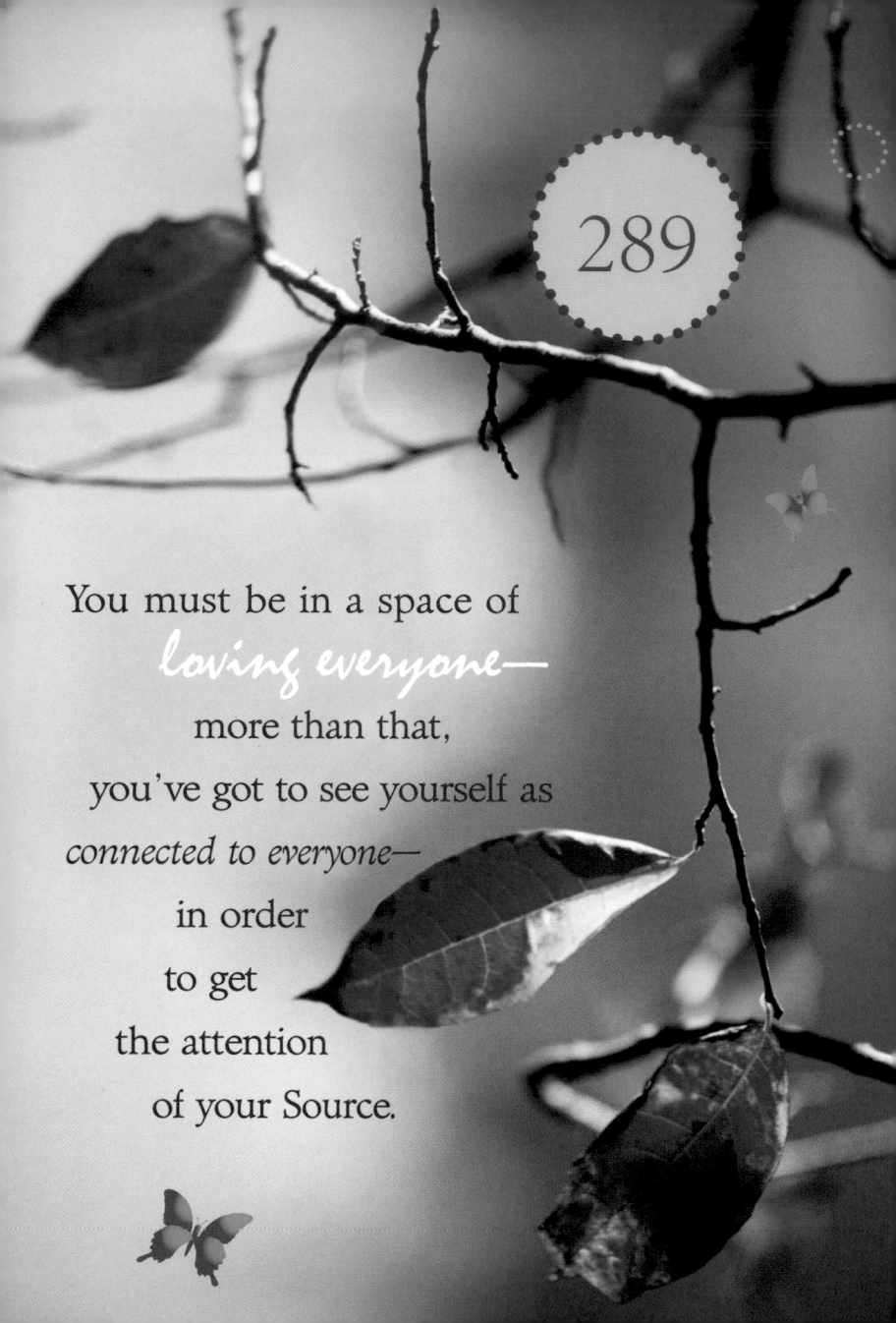

289

You must be in a space of
loving everyone—
more than that,
you've got to see yourself as
connected to everyone—
in order
to get
the attention
of your Source.

290

Ultimately,
make it your goal to unashamedly
slay your ego
while you're still
in your body.

291

When you're *in-Spirit*,

you have a

feeling of contentment,

but more than that,

you experience joy.

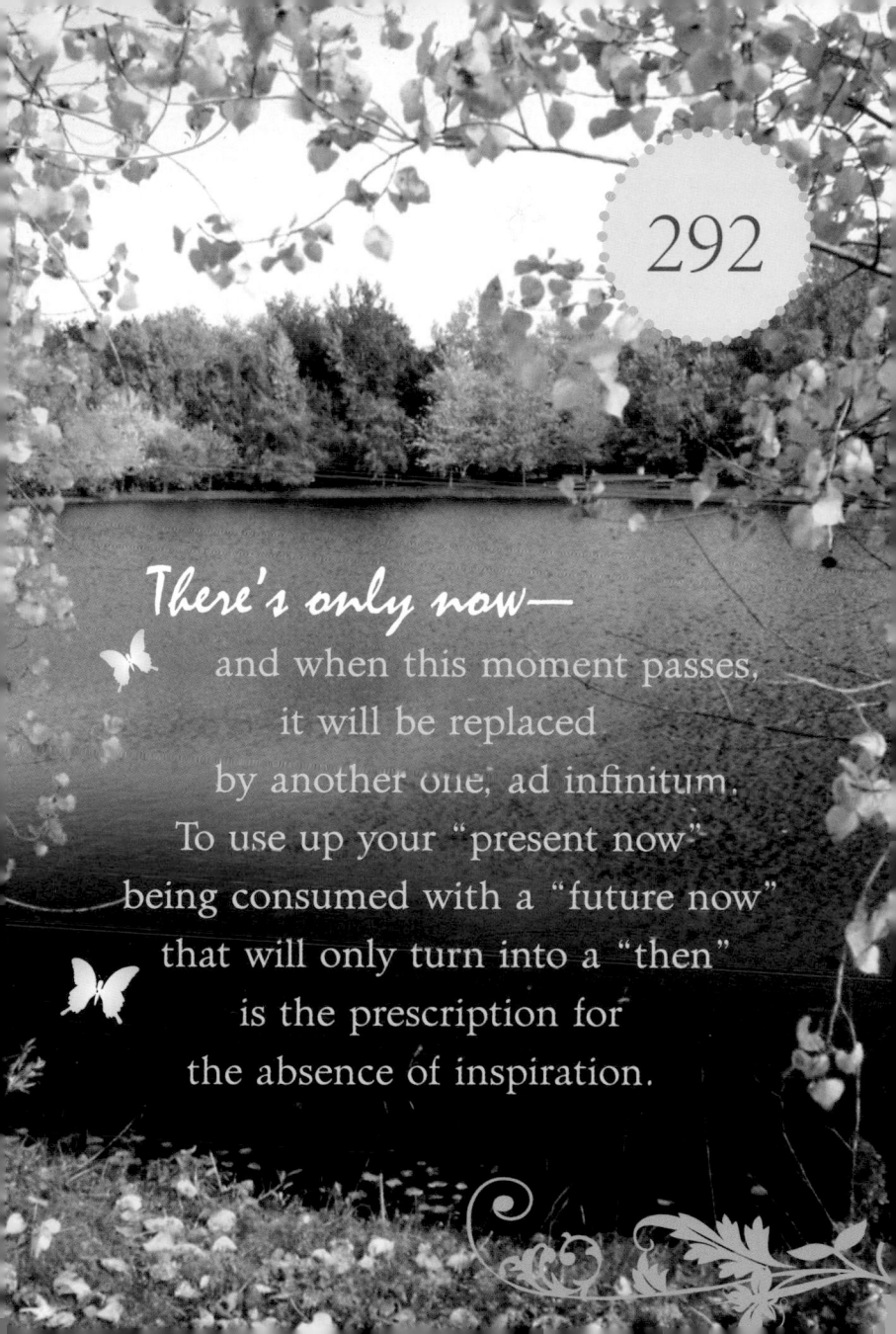

292

There's only now—
and when this moment passes,
it will be replaced
by another one, ad infinitum.
To use up your "present now"
being consumed with a "future now"
that will only turn into a "then"
is the prescription for
the absence of inspiration.

293

Something that seems
to come from afar,
where you allow yourself to be moved
by a force that's more powerful
than your ego and all of its illusions,

is inspiration.

294

Trust in the Intelligence

that beats your heart

50 or 60 times every minute
and at the same time turns planet Earth
once every 24 hours,
keeps the planets aligned,
and creates every
millisecond.

295

You must trust
that inspiration is already present
in your life—
it only eludes you
because you've disconnected
in some way
from the Spirit
that was
and always will be
your essence.

You may believe that inspiration is something that arrives in some mysterious way that's beyond your control, but it's clearly best to *rely exclusively on your decisions* to act in ways that will intensify your awareness of Spirit.

296

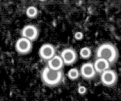

Suffering the
consequences of living
according to someone else's wishes
doesn't make any sense;
rather, you need to
oppose the external
opinions that try to force you
to be what you're not
intended to be.

297

298

Being inspired
is truly *being like your Source.*

If you're not, then your Source
is politely waiting for you
to do something
as simple as
change
your
mind.

299

What prevents you

from seeing yourself as containing

"the essence of God"

and knowing that you're of "noble birth"?

Only ego.

A non-ego-based point of view

must be firmly in place

on the journey

to an inspired,

passionate life.

300

As the great Indian sage
Ramana Maharshi once remarked,
"There is no goal to be reached.
There is nothing to be attained.
You are the Self.
You exist always."
This is true inspiration.

301

This is clearly
a purposeful Universe,
with an Intelligence
supporting its creation and
continuing evolution—
and you're a piece of
that Intelligence
by virtue of
having emerged
from it.

302

The desire to
*find your way
to inspiration*
involves creating
a vision of living *in-Spirit*
100 percent
of the time.

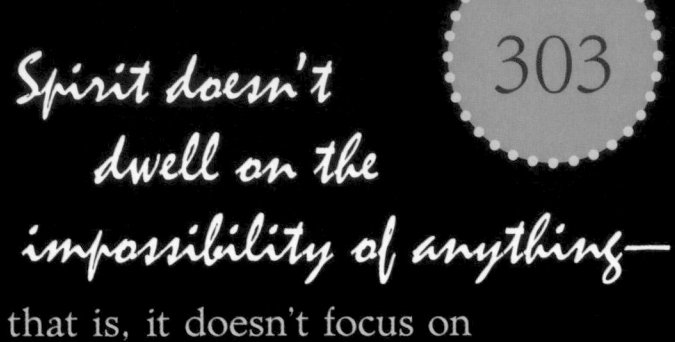

Spirit doesn't dwell on the impossibility of anything—

that is, it doesn't focus on

not being able to create,

on things not working out,

on expecting the worst,

or on being stuck

in place.

303

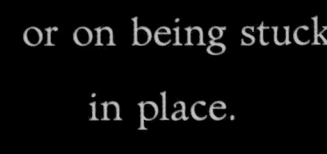

304

Extend love outward.
This can take the form
of a silent blessing
toward someone you might
have previously judged,
a loving greeting,
a kind remark,
or a thought wishing
the highest good
for all concerned.

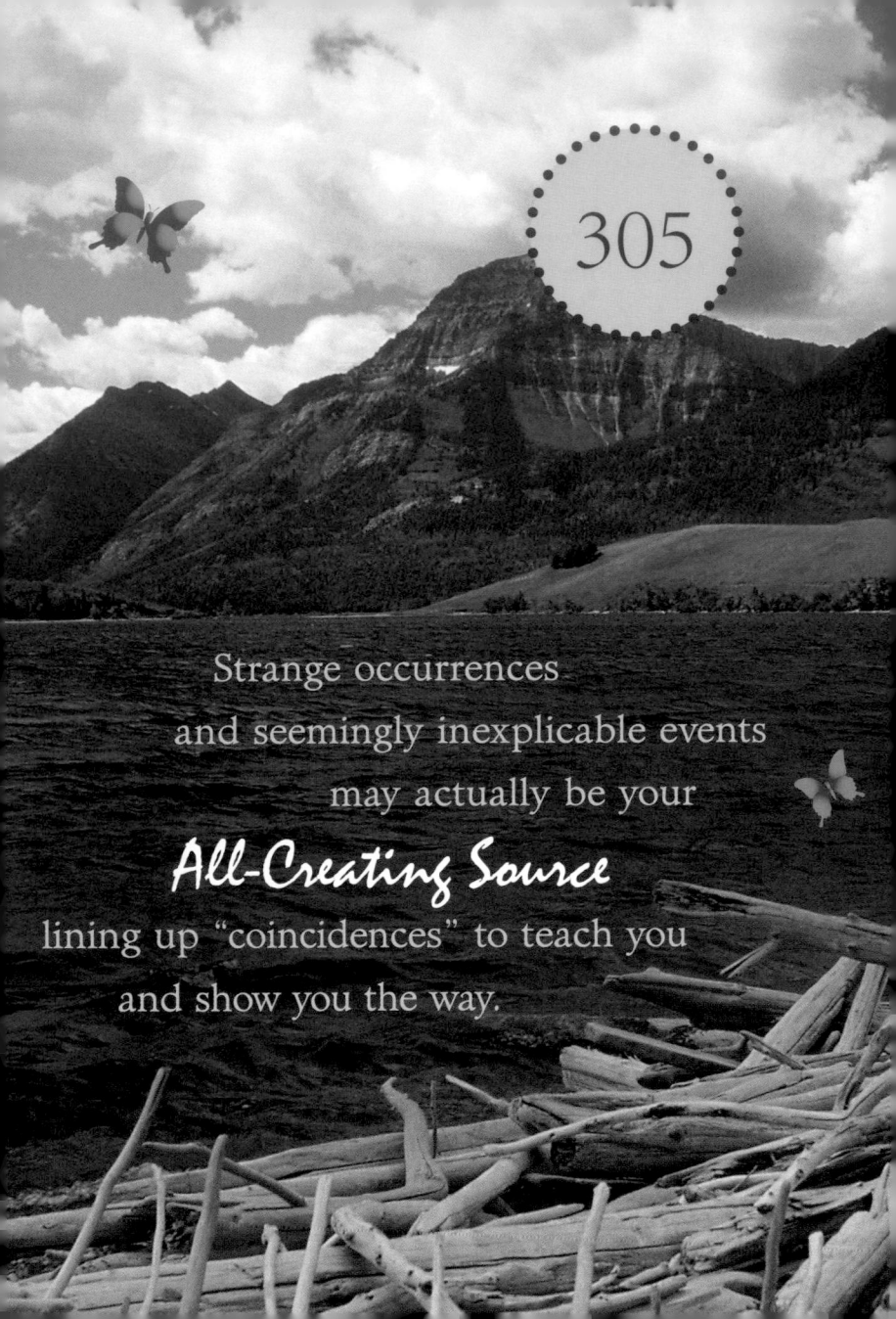

305

Strange occurrences
and seemingly inexplicable events
may actually be your

All-Creating Source

lining up "coincidences" to teach you

and show you the way.

In ways that

you don't

readily comprehend now,

when you were in your

place of origin

you knew what you were

coming here to accomplish,

and you participated in

setting this

life process

in motion.

Living *in-Spirit* means
that you see your body with all
of its unique characteristics
and feel thankful for
the perfect temple
that's temporarily housing
your true
"primary existence."

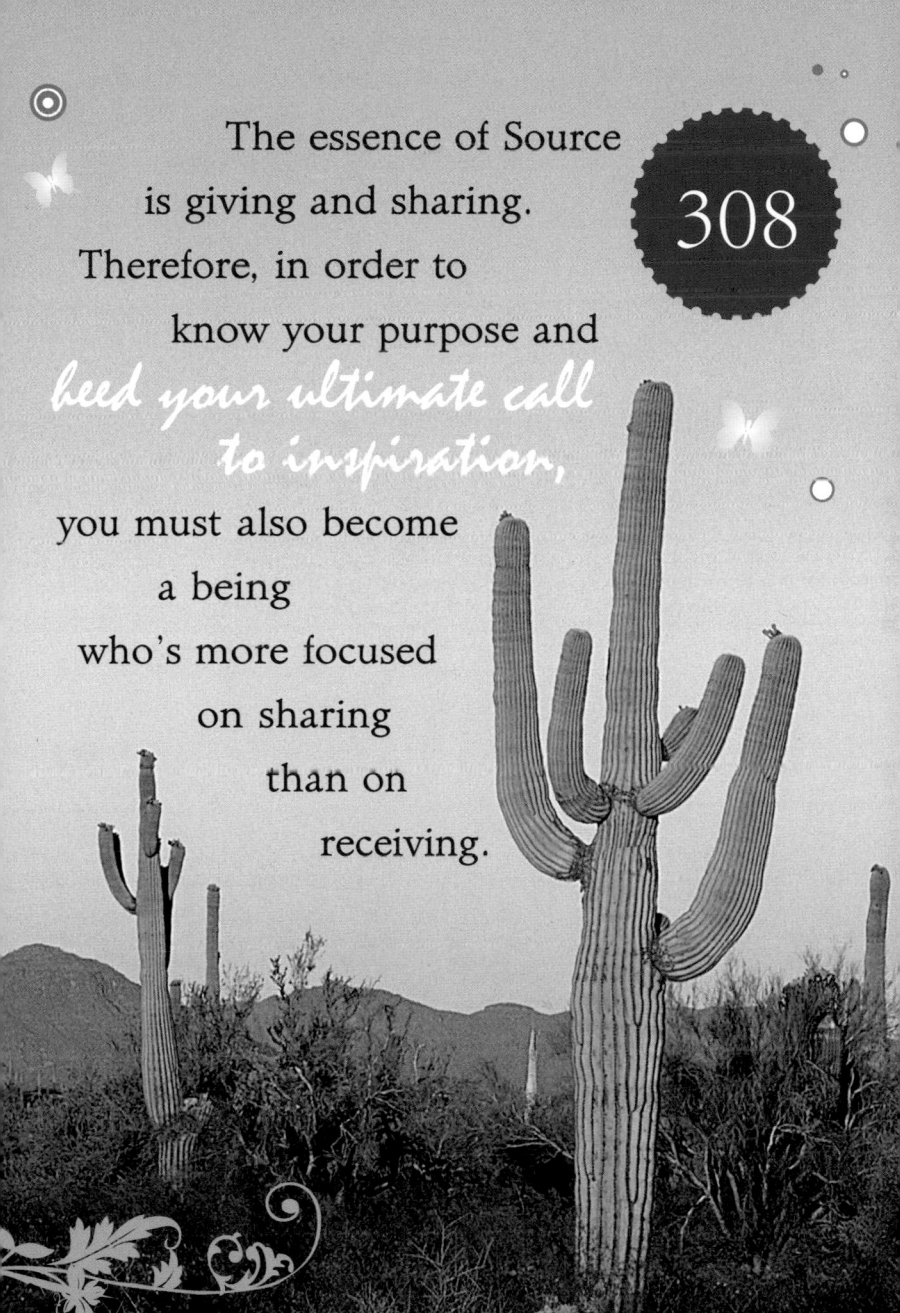

The essence of Source
is giving and sharing.
Therefore, in order to
know your purpose and
*heed your ultimate call
to inspiration,*
you must also become
a being
who's more focused
on sharing
than on
receiving.

308

309

When you're living *in-Spirit,*

you can feel inspired

by doing virtually

anything.

310

During the months that
you lived in your mother's womb,
it's safe to say
that you were *in-Spirit*—
you were allowing Spirit
to perfectly align
without any effort
on your part.

311

Throughout your life,
you continue
your development
outside of the womb,
wherein you rely
on the energy of creation
to fuel the light
of inspiration
within you.

312

Make your
primary goal to stay
in this consciousness
and enjoy every moment,
putting into practice
what you agreed to
when you were *in-Spirit*
before becoming
the particle
that began this
glorious
journey.

313

Inspiration flowing
through you is a
messenger from the
realm of your nonphysical
self, from where you were
before you entered this
visible world of form.

314

You can watch
as some things enter your life
and others leave, all the while
remaining in-Spirit,
knowing that all of those things
have nothing to do
with your state of inspiration.

315

As you move more deeply into Spirit,

you cease to be guided

by the ego demands of others or yourself.

You surrender to

the always-present Force

that urges you

to be in a

blissful state
of inspiration.

316

Practice sharing
anonymously.
*The goal is
to be at one
with the Creator,*
and It isn't looking
for credit, a reward,
or even a thank-you.

317

Whenever you find yourself
"wanting more,"
the solution is to do more
for society, for humanity,
or for the environment.
Any act of sharing as a response to
your wants leads
to feeling inspired.

Your job is to

understand and accept

that all of the things that

show up in your life, which you

often find contradictory or

troublesome, are there

because you've attracted them

. . . and you need to deal with these

obstacles in order to clear

an opening for

your true

purpose to

emerge.

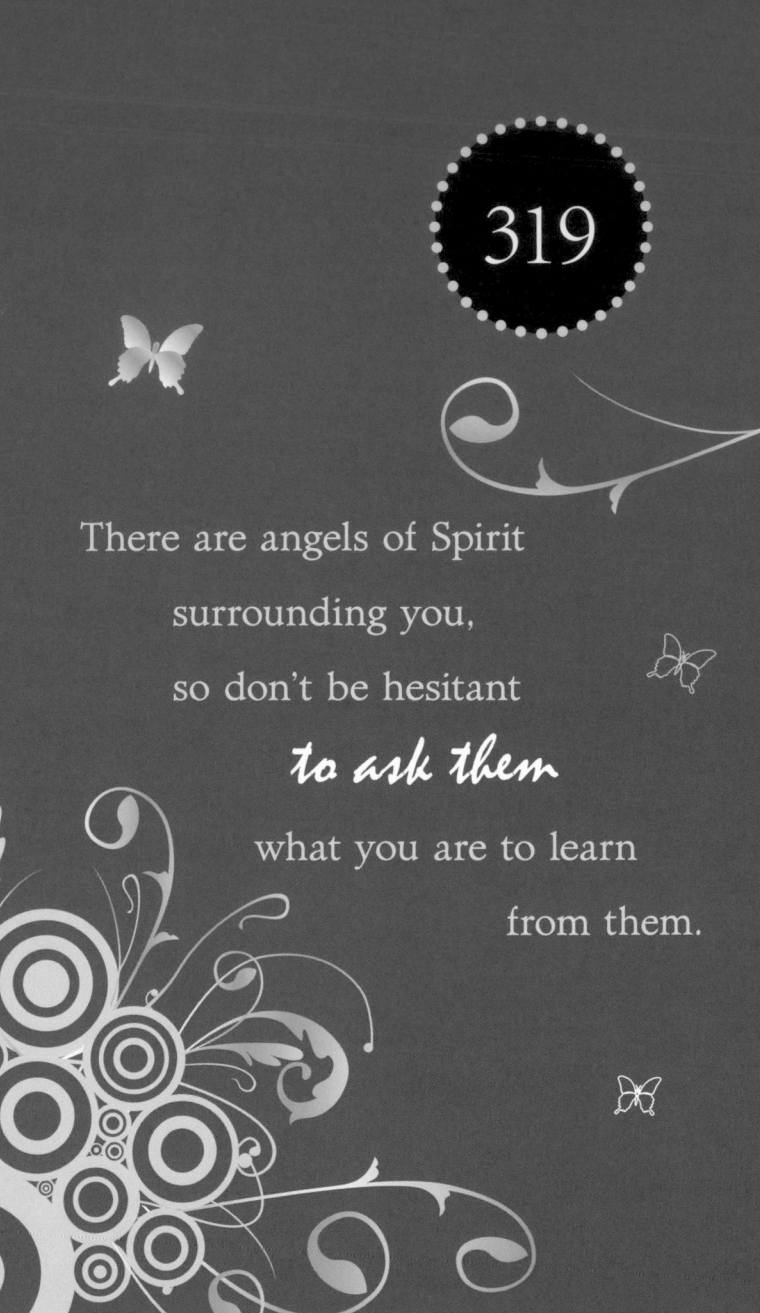

319

There are angels of Spirit

surrounding you,

so don't be hesitant

to ask them

what you are to learn

from them.

320

Your abilities are
as limitless as
God's
because you're
a distinct portion
of the
essence
of Him.

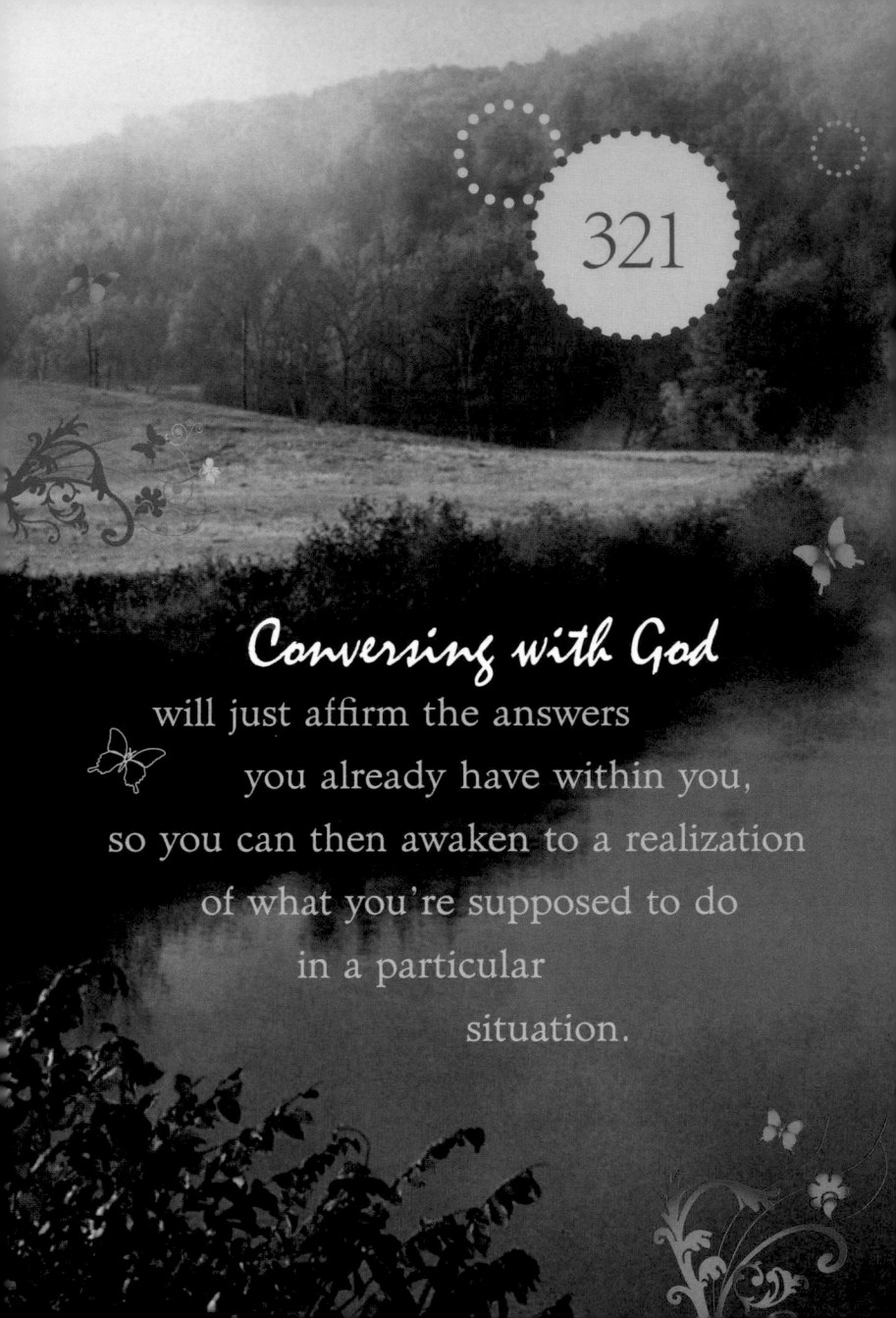

321

Conversing with God
will just affirm the answers
you already have within you,
so you can then awaken to a realization
of what you're supposed to do
in a particular
situation.

322

Keep in mind that
as one of
God's glorious thoughts,
you've originated
out of an energy field
that knows only possibility,
so stay in vibrational harmony
with this idea.

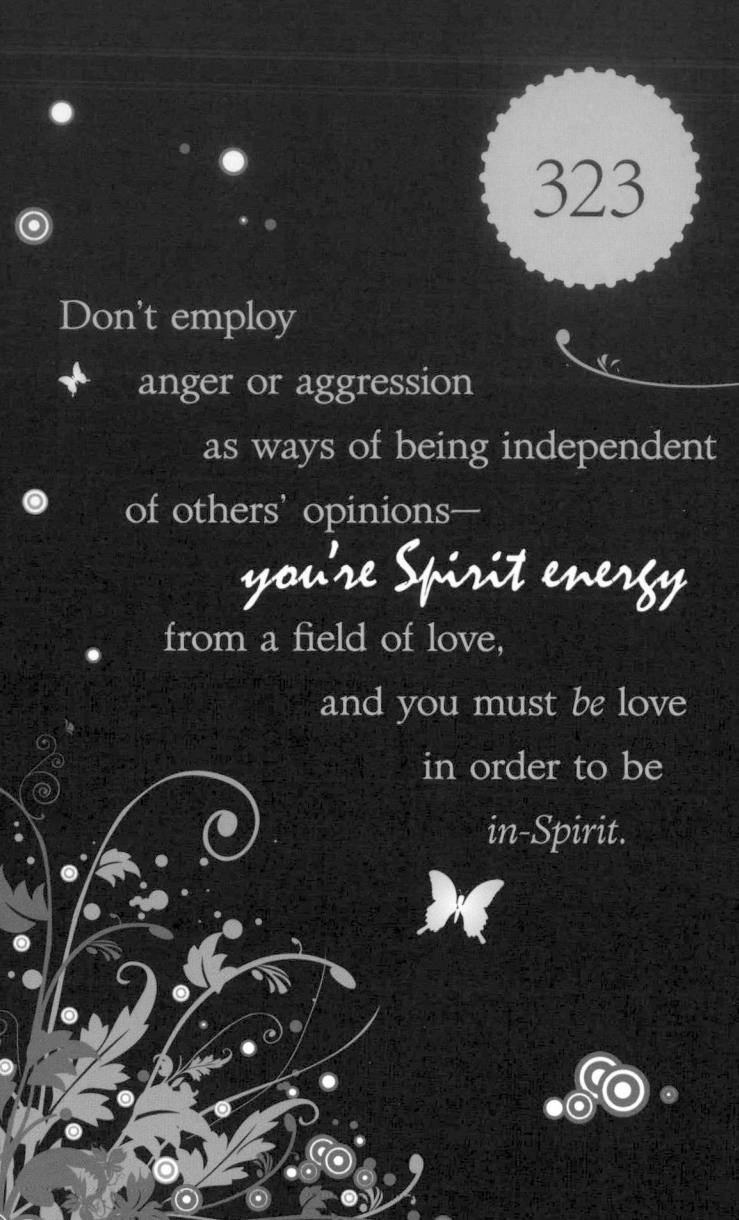

323

Don't employ
anger or aggression
as ways of being independent
of others' opinions—
you're Spirit energy
from a field of love,
and you must *be* love
in order to be
in-Spirit.

324

You're here in
your perfect body
for your time here
in this incarnation,
and it's a living, breathing miracle
in every way.

325

Be Here Now is more
than a great book title by Ram Dass;
it's the essence of inspiration.
Being in the now is the way
to remove anxiety, stress,
and even some illnesses.

326

Give yourself the
time and quiet space
to enter into dialogue
with your Source.
The answers you seek
will come rushing
toward you when you're
*in authentic
communication.*

327

The mere fact

that you're interested

and excited about doing something

is all the evidence you need

that inspiration

is right in front of you,

begging you

to pay attention

to it.

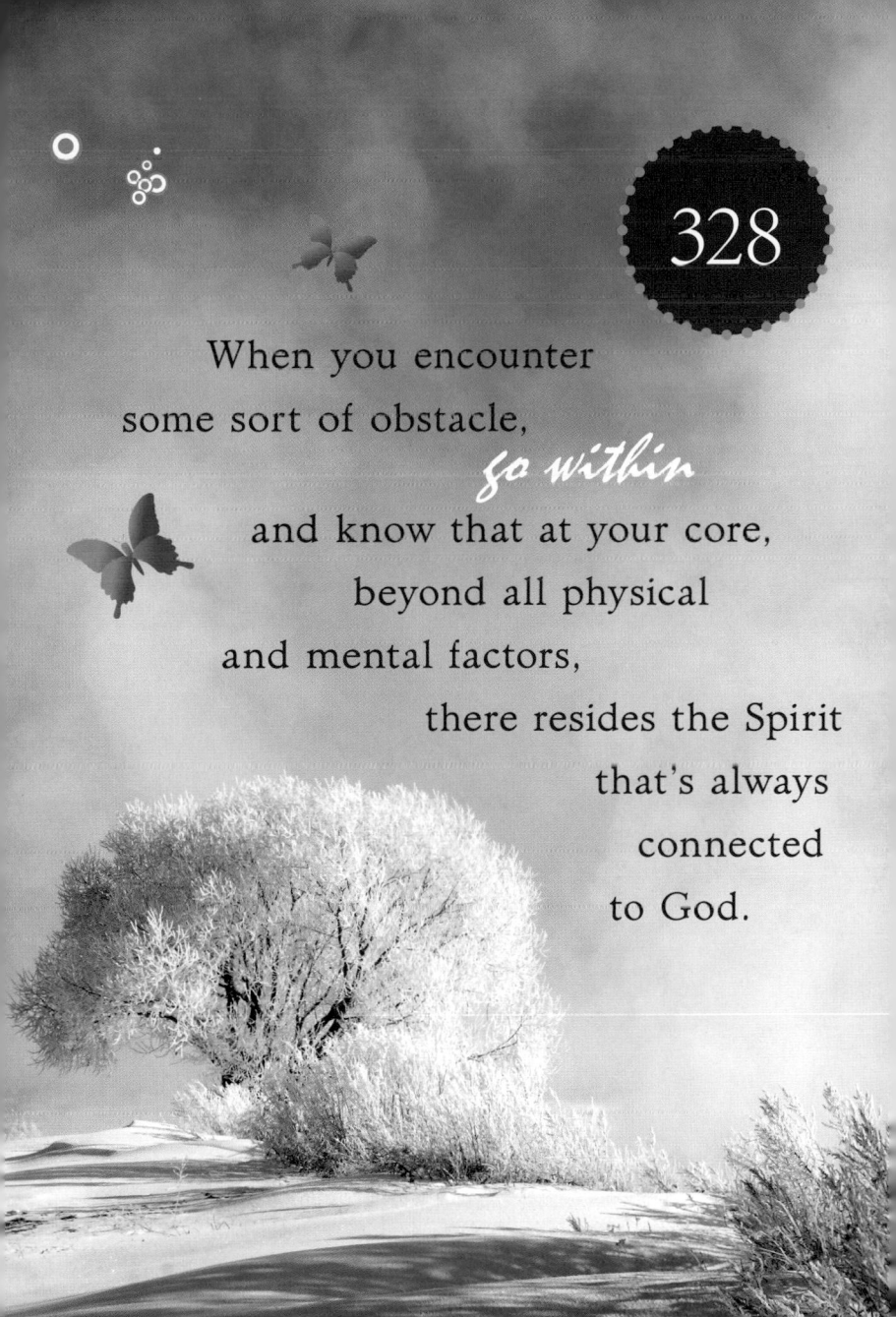

328

When you encounter
some sort of obstacle,
go within
and know that at your core,
beyond all physical
and mental factors,
there resides the Spirit
that's always
connected
to God.

329

Who am I?
is the "big question."
The *answer* to it is:
I'm a unique portion
of the essence of God.
I originated <u>in-Spirit,</u>
yet I've forgotten
this fundamental truth.

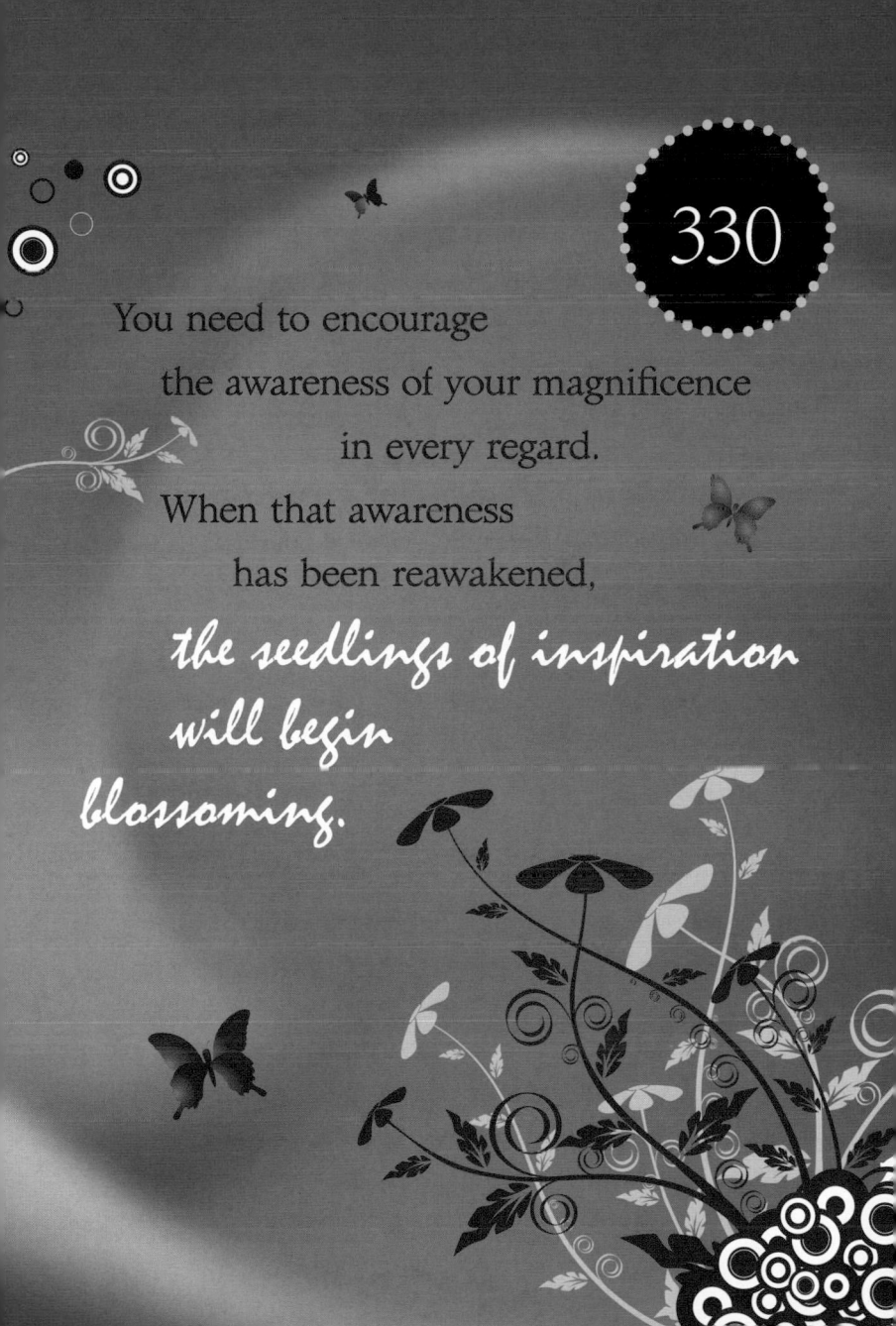

330

You need to encourage
the awareness of your magnificence
in every regard.
When that awareness
has been reawakened,
the seedlings of inspiration
will begin
blossoming.

331

When you're being directed

by your "Senior Partner,"

the end result in any situation

takes care of itself,

particularly since you

see the end result

in your mind,

and you use your

present moments

in harmony

with that vision.

By trusting in *your* inner vision, you're trusting the same Wisdom *that created you.*

332

333

Being *in-Spirit*

is the place where you

connect to the invisible reality

that ultimately directs you

toward your calling.

334

You aren't required
to give to, pay homage to,
or do anything for God.
It's *your* demands that
distance you from feeling inspired—
so you need to let go
of them and extend yourself
in an attitude of sharing.

335

Remember this simple truth:
The answer to *how* is *yes*.
You may never know
exactly *how* you're going
to accomplish
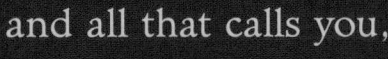
the feeling of inspiration,
but by saying *yes* to life
and all that calls you,
the *how* will
take care of itself.

336

The moment
you catch yourself
excluding someone
or having a
judgmental thought,
say the words
in-Spirit to yourself.
Then make a silent
effort *to shift*
that thought
to match up with
Source energy.

337

Be gentle and forgiving
with yourself,
abandon any and all shame,
and refuse to engage
in any self-repudiation.

338

In an infinite Universe,
there's no time restriction
on how many lifetimes
you get.

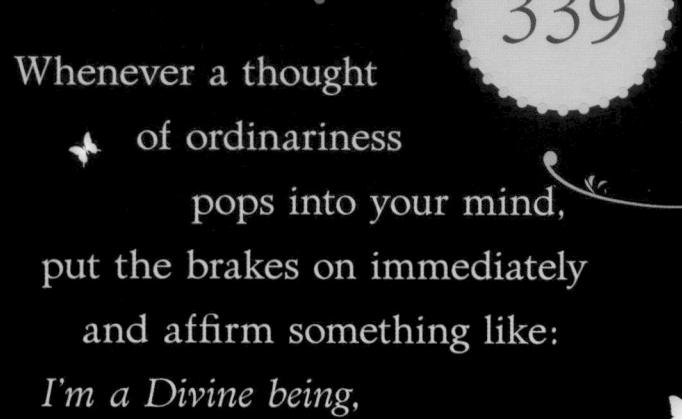

339

Whenever a thought
of ordinariness
pops into your mind,
put the brakes on immediately
and affirm something like:
I'm a Divine being,
a distinct portion
of the essence of God.
This silent reminder
will do more
for your inspiration
than a thousand
books and
a hundred seminars.

Inspiration can be cultivated and be *a driving enthusiasm* *throughout* life, rather than showing up every now and then and just as mysteriously disappearing, seemingly independent of your desire.

341

In order to achieve
*a reunion with
your ultimate calling,*
you need to emulate
the clear, uncomplicated world
of Spirit.

342

Continually remind yourself
of the physical
and metaphysical truth
that there's no place
anywhere in this Universe
*that's devoid
of Spirit.*

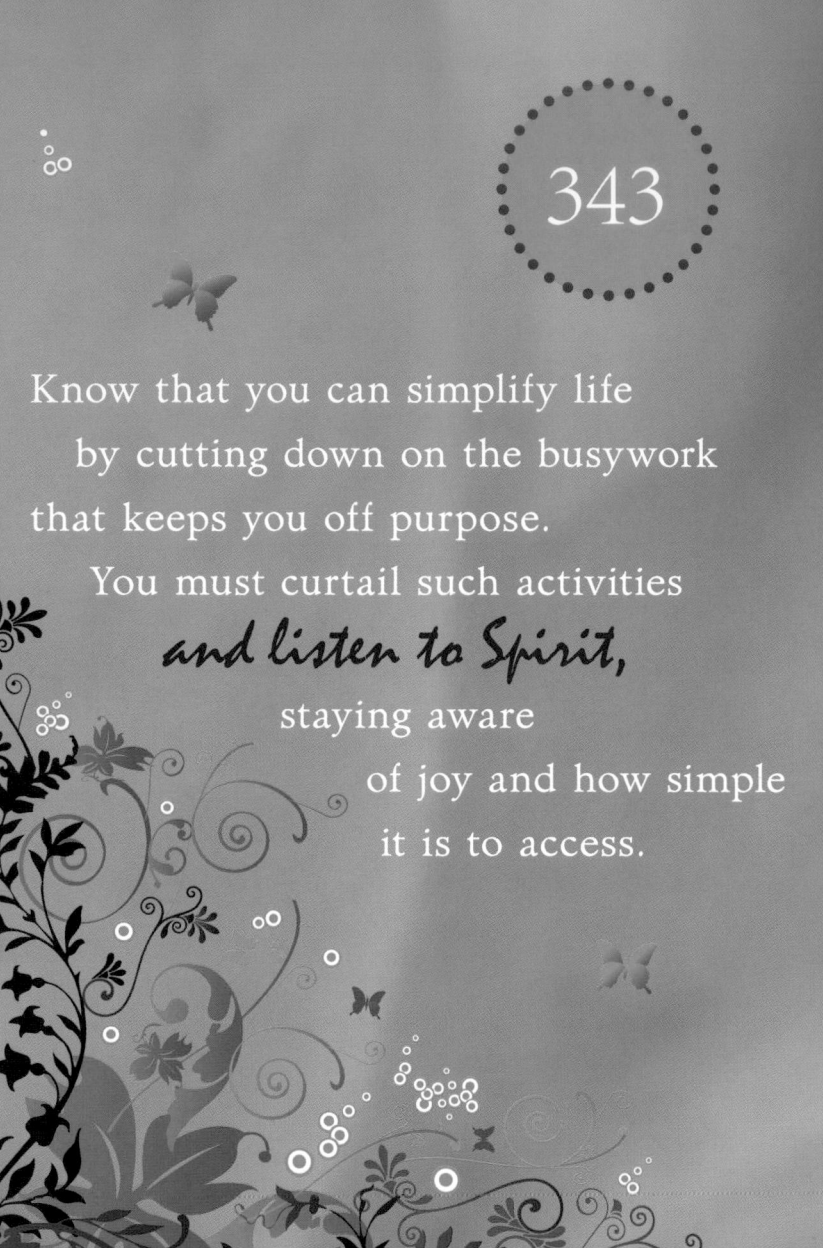

343

Know that you can simplify life
by cutting down on the busywork
that keeps you off purpose.
You must curtail such activities
and listen to Spirit,
staying aware
of joy and how simple
it is to access.

There's perfect timing
in the Universe,
and your arrival on Earth was a
part of that synchronicity.
In other words, you were
an idea of God's
whose time
had come.

344

345

It's important to
*match your desires
to your expectations.*
You need to see
everything you
want arriving . . .
and know that
it can't be stopped.

346

You get what
you think about,
whether you want it or not!
*So be careful
what you think about.*

347

When you enter
the energy field
of someone who's
connected to Spirit,
you find yourself not only
forsaking your uninspired ways,
but also
*converting to their
higher energy.*

348

When you make the decision
to become a being of sharing,
and practice keeping your thoughts
*harmonized with
Spirit energy*
on a daily basis,
your purpose will not only find you,
it will *chase after* you
wherever you go.

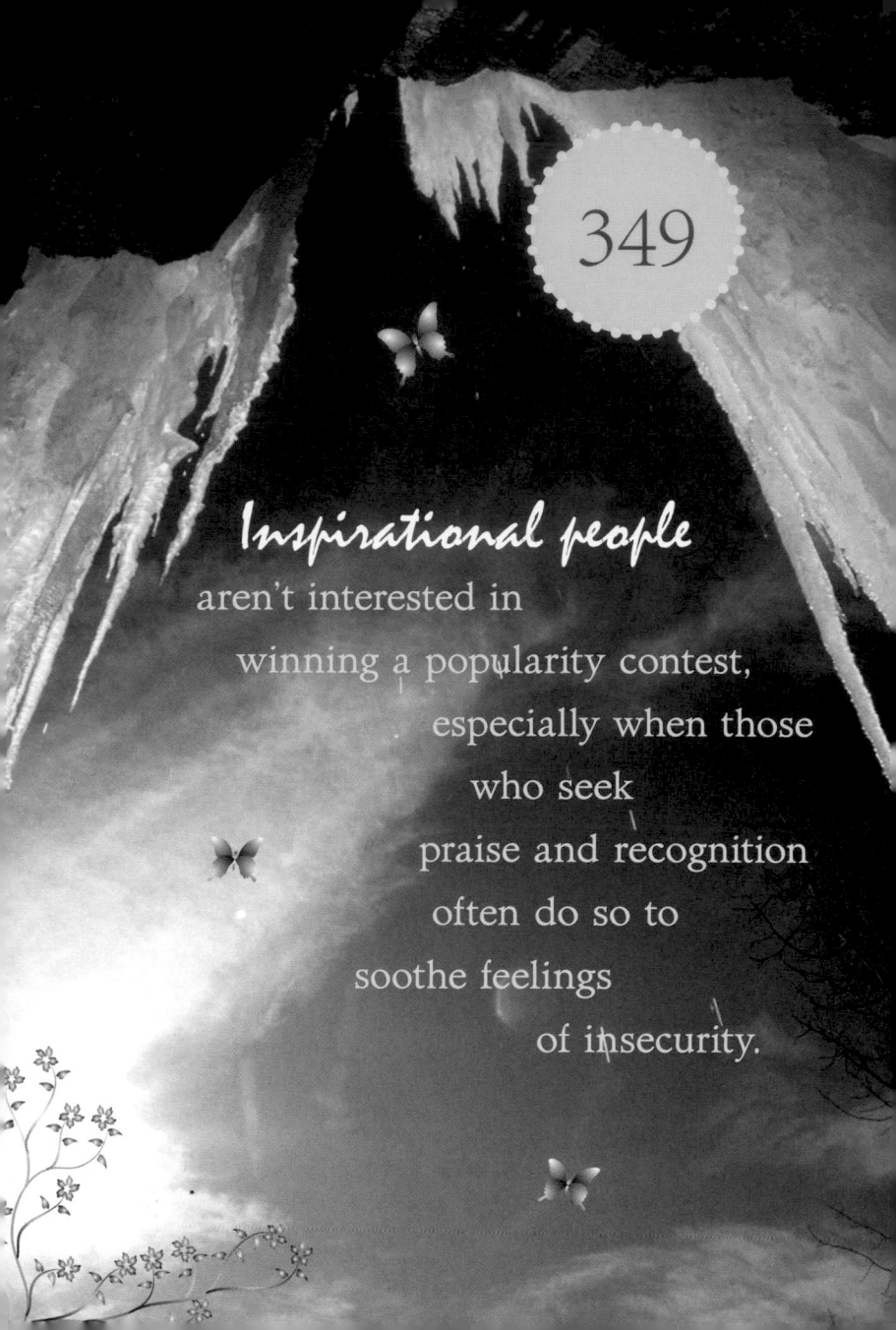

349

Inspirational people
aren't interested in
winning a popularity contest,
especially when those
who seek
praise and recognition
often do so to
soothe feelings
of insecurity.

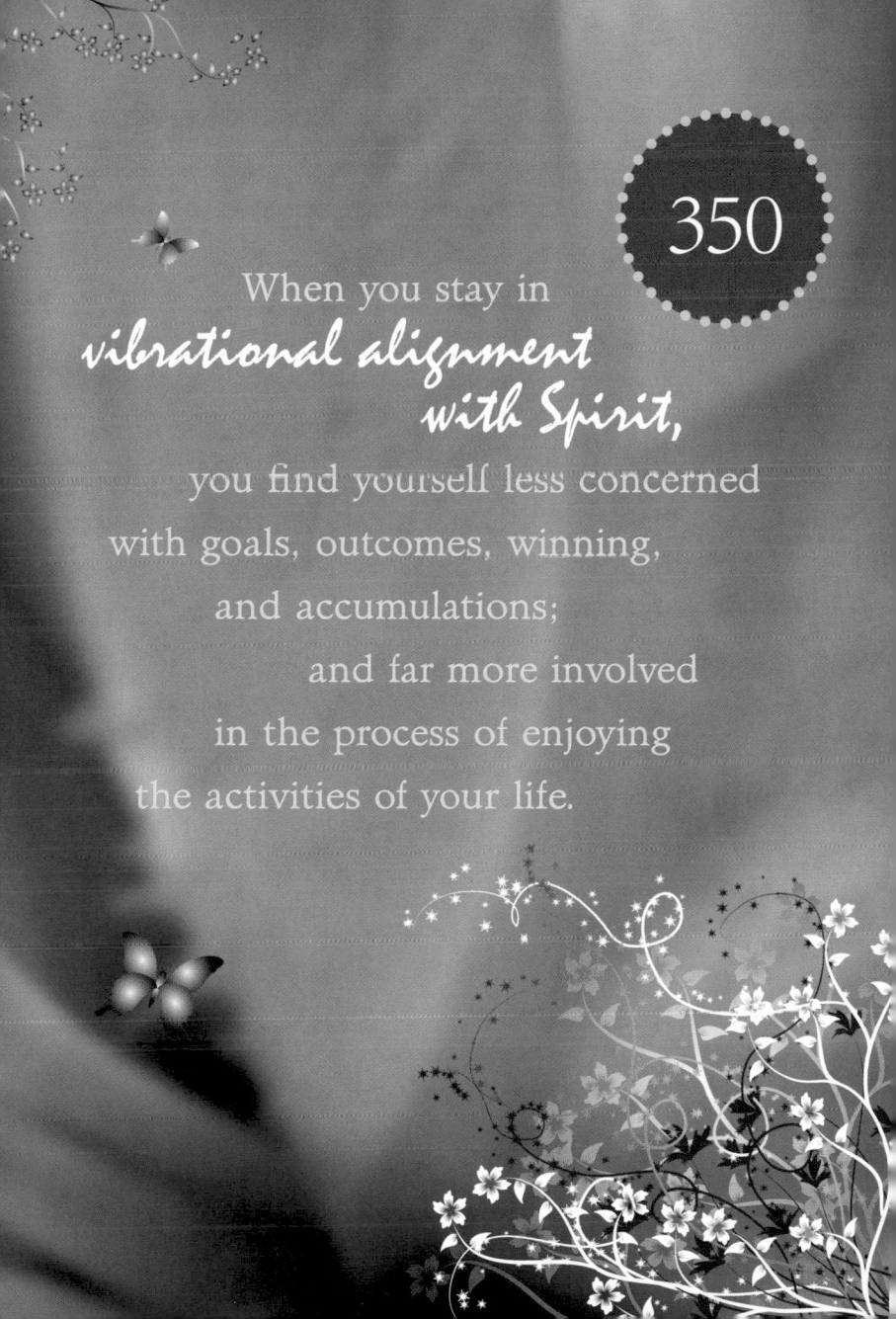

350

When you stay in
*vibrational alignment
with Spirit,*
you find yourself less concerned
with goals, outcomes, winning,
and accumulations;
and far more involved
in the process of enjoying
the activities of your life.

351

The energy of your thoughts

determines whether or not
you're living at an inspired level,
so any doubt in your ability to
manifest your desire or to receive
spiritual guidance is
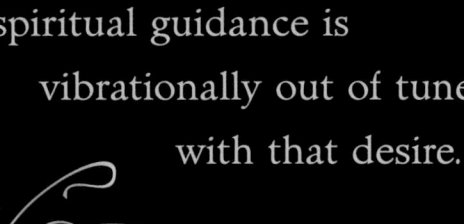
vibrationally out of tune
with that desire.

352

Trust your own intuition—
no one else has to agree
with you or even understand you.
Remember, your goal
is to feel good (God).

353

You always have the
power within you
to shift into a
peaceful mode.

354

Note that any- and everything
that keeps you from

appreciating your
spiritual Source

is an impediment.
This particularly includes
relying on someone else or
some organization without examining
the truths that they insist
you believe in.

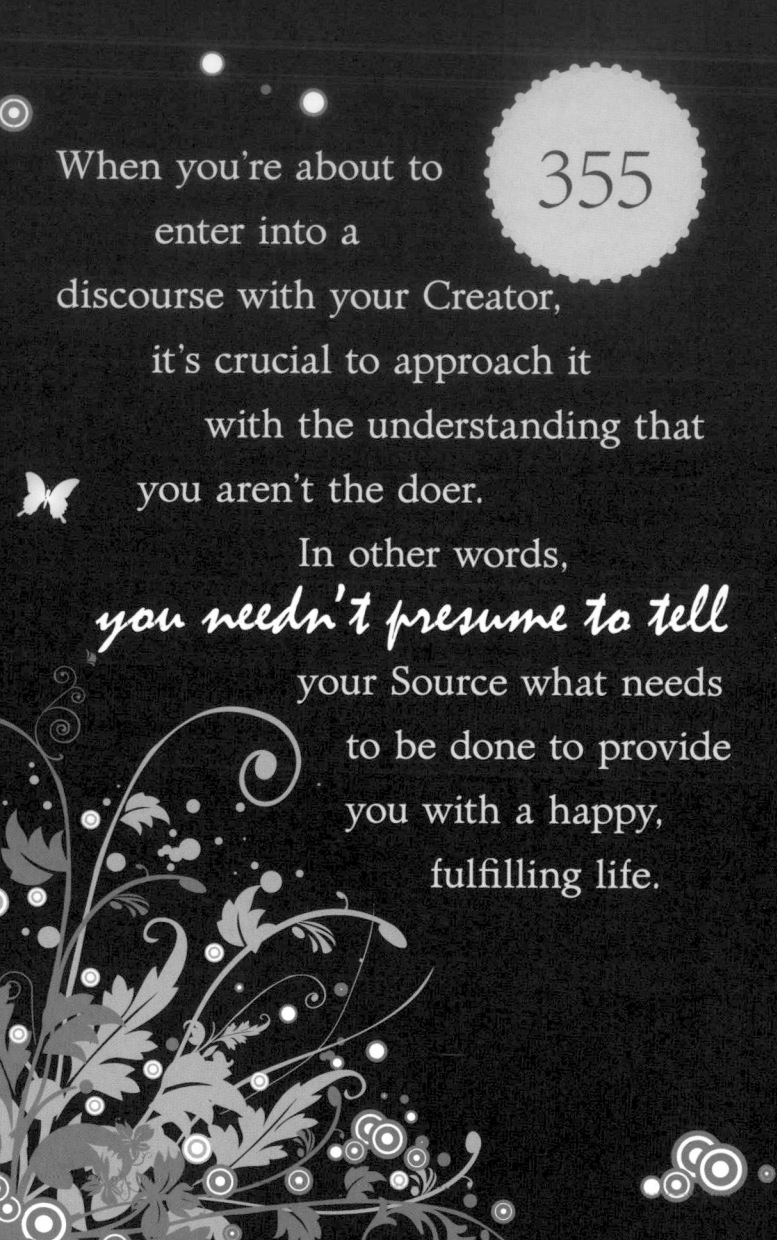

When you're about to enter into a discourse with your Creator, it's crucial to approach it with the understanding that you aren't the doer. In other words, *you needn't presume to tell* your Source what needs to be done to provide you with a happy, fulfilling life.

355

356

If you make this an
inner mantra:
I intend to feel good,
you can picture yourself
experiencing joy
regardless of
what's going on
around you.

357

Along with praying or communing
with your Source with peace in your heart,

you must "be still."

This means taking time to get
quiet before meditating,
and also monitoring your breathing.

You must know that absolutely no one else truly knows and feels what you're here to accomplish, so you need to *give yourself permission to hear* your inner guidance and ignore pressure from others.

358

359

No matter what your religion,
whenever you want
*to communicate with
your Source of Being,*
you must do so
without malice
or hatred
in your heart.

The one Source of
all-encompassing love
knows nothing of boundaries;
differing customs; geographic
divisions; family splits; or
differences in race, creed, sex,
and so on—It only knows
love for all.

360

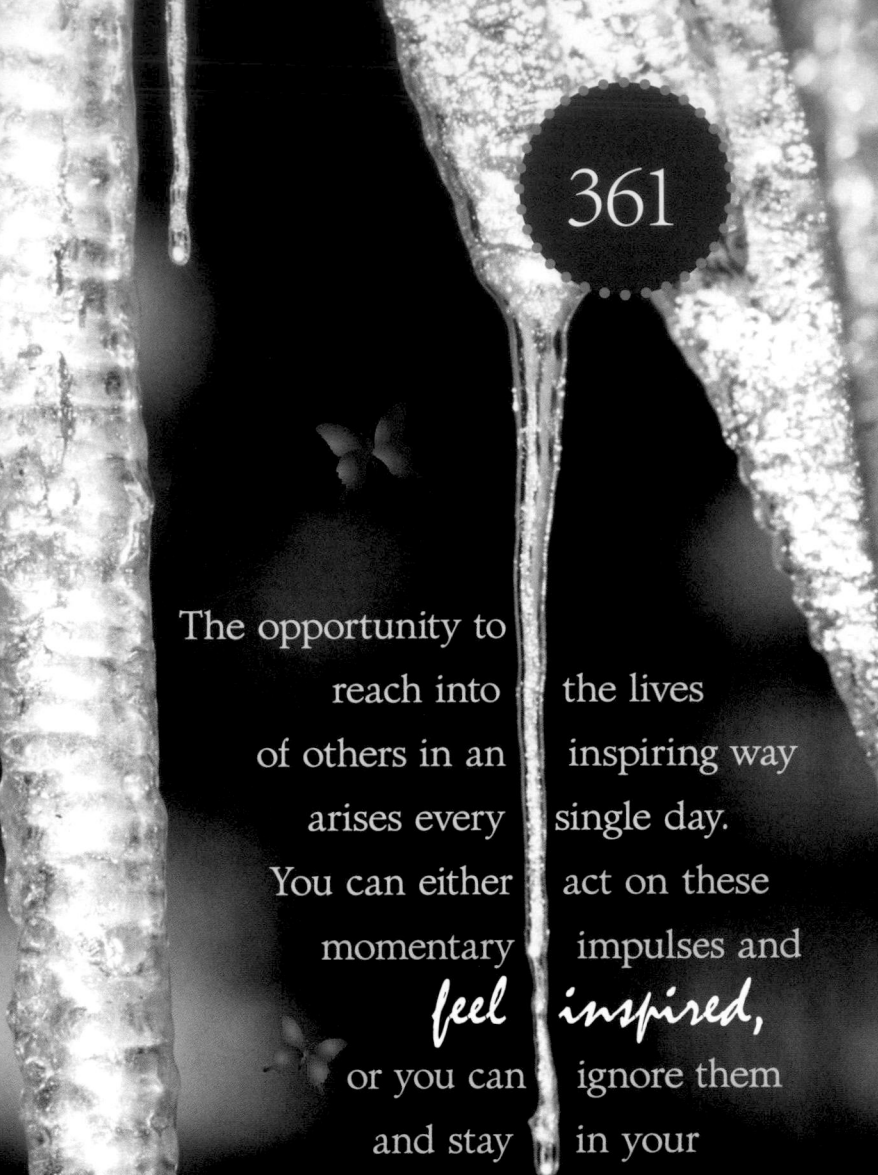

361

The opportunity to
reach into the lives
of others in an inspiring way
arises every single day.
You can either act on these
momentary impulses and
feel inspired,
or you can ignore them
and stay in your
ego-dominated world.

By writing down

your intentions

and having them

readily available to refer to,

you nurture

the inspirational energy

to follow through

on your interests.

362

363

Being stimulated by something
is the clue to a thought that's
connected to your calling—
and that thought
is a vibration
of energy
in this vast Universe.

You're in a body
that has a natural
tendency toward health
*and can overcome
almost anything*
if you allow it to perform
its own
magic.

364

Be on the lookout

for opportunities to be

a source of inspiration,

just by being an example.

By demonstrating

your own connection to Spirit,

you inspire others, and you'll

feel inspiration flowing through you.

365

ABOUT THE AUTHOR

Wayne W. Dyer, Ph.D., is an internationally renowned author and speaker in the field of self-development. He's the author of 30 books, has created many audio programs and videos, and has appeared on thousands of television and radio shows. His books *Manifest Your Destiny, Wisdom of the Ages, There's a Spiritual Solution to Every Problem,* and *The New York Times* bestsellers *10 Secrets for Success and Inner Peace, The Power of Intention, Inspiration,* and *Change Your Thoughts—Change Your Life* have all been featured as National Public Television specials.

Wayne holds a doctorate in educational counseling from Wayne State University and was an associate professor at St. John's University in New York.

Website: **www.DrWayneDyer.com**

NOTES

NOTES

NOTES

NOTES

NOTES

NOTES

HAY HOUSE TITLES OF RELATED INTEREST

You Can Heal Your Life,
the movie, starring Louise L. Hay & Friends
(available as a 1-DVD program and an expanded 2-DVD set)
Watch the trailer at: **www.LouiseHayMovie.com**

Healing Words from the Angels,
by Doreen Virtue, Ph.D.

Never Mind Success . . . Go for Greatness!
by Tavis Smiley

101 Ways to Jump-Start Your Intuition,
by John Holland

The Present Moment,
by Louise L. Hay

Vitamins for the Soul,
by Sonia Choquette

• • •

All of the above are available at your local bookstore,
or may be ordered by visiting:

Hay House USA: **www.hayhouse.com**®
Hay House Australia: **www.hayhouse.com.au**
Hay House UK: **www.hayhouse.co.uk**
Hay House South Africa: **www.hayhouse.co.za**
Hay House India: **www.hayhouse.co.in**

We hope you enjoyed this Hay House Lifestyles book.
If you would like to receive a free catalog featuring additional
Hay House books and products, or if you would like information
about the Hay Foundation, please contact:

Hay House, Inc., P.O. Box 5100, Carlsbad, CA 92018-5100

(760) 431-7695 or (800) 654-5126
(760) 431-6948 (fax) or (800) 650-5115 (fax)
www.hayhouse.com® • www.hayfoundation.org

• • •

Published and distributed in Australia by:
Hay House Australia Pty. Ltd., 18/36 Ralph St., Alexandria NSW 2015
Phone: 612-9669-4299 • *Fax:* 612-9669-4144 • www.hayhouse.com.au

Published and distributed in the United Kingdom by:
Hay House UK, Ltd., 292B Kensal Rd., London W10 5BE
Phone: 44-20-8962-1230 • *Fax:* 44-20-8962-1239 • www.hayhouse.co.uk

Published and distributed in the Republic of South Africa by:
Hay House SA (Pty), Ltd., P.O. Box 990, Witkoppen 2068
Phone/Fax: 27-11-467-8904 • orders@psdprom.co.za • www.hayhouse.co.za

Published in India by:
Hay House Publishers India, Muskaan Complex, Plot No. 3, B-2, Vasant Kunj,
New Delhi 110 070 • *Phone:* 91-11-4176-1620 • *Fax:* 91-11-4176-1630 • www.hayhouse.co.in

Distributed in Canada by:
Raincoast, 9050 Shaughnessy St., Vancouver, B.C. V6P 6E5
Phone: (604) 323-7100 • *Fax:* (604) 323-2600 • www.raincoast.com

• • •

Tune in to **HayHouseRadio.com**® for the best in inspirational talk radio featuring
top Hay House authors! And, sign up via the Hay House USA Website to receive
the Hay House online newsletter and stay informed about what's going on with your
favorite authors. You'll receive bimonthly announcements about: Discounts and
Offers, Special Events, Product Highlights, Free Excerpts, Giveaways, and more!
www.hayhouse.com®

• • •